REDEFINING RETIREMENT
FOR A NEW GENERATION

ON TASK PUBLISHING

On Task Publishing

ISBN: 978-0-9842774-1-4
Library of Congress Control Number: 2009910540
Printed in the United States of America

Redefining

RETIREMENT
FOR A NEW GENERATION

**Saving Your Retirement
in a Turbulent World**

Robert J. Krakower

ON TASK PUBLISHING

CONTENTS

PART TWO:
SHELTER FROM THE STORM:
THE REALITY OF RISK AND THE
FIGHT FOR RETIREMENT

I dedicate this book to
Lori, Samantha, and Nicholas
I am proud to have you on my journey through life

FOREWORD

It is truly an honor for me to write this foreword to *Redefining Retirement*. I am convinced this book will help save your retirement in the turbulent 21st Century. As you read through it, you will see how the conventional view of retirement is outdated, and that the retirement and income planning of the past, along with increased life expectancy, and the rise of 401(k) plans replacing pensions, means old definitions no longer apply.

Robert J. Krakower has combined his 20 years of experience in consulting, professional speaking and training, with current research and the current economic turbulence, to create a book that is credible, fact-filled and personal, and written in a conversational style. Robert offers amazing insight into the new, game-changing realities of the "Retirement Perfect Storm" that is headed for America's retirement system, and that the majority of people are unaware is coming. He lays out an unflinching guide to the opportunities awaiting anyone heading into retirement, as well as exposes the pitfalls and hazards to a secure retirement that the financial media continues to mask in an endless fog of useless information and unfulfilled promises.

You will gain insight into a hidden world of financial knowledge as Robert pulls back the curtain and reveals the true state of the mutual fund industry. You will discover the real reason why your mutual funds perform so poorly, see how your 401(k) plan stacks up against the ideal retirement plan, understand the pros and cons of the "buy-and-hold" slogan for modern investing, and learn to apply the steps necessary to shelter and protect your retirement dreams and financial goals, thus saving your retirement in a turbulent world.

At McNally Wealth Management, we stand wholeheartedly behind Robert's call to arms. Read this book thoughtfully, take notes, remembering that the "Journey of a Lifetime, begins with a single step." Then share what you've discovered with your family, friends and colleagues and then take action and experience what countless others have when you become a member of the Redefined Generation.

We are here to serve you,

Patrick D. McNally, AIF
Founder and President
McNally Wealth Management
Redding, California

PART ONE

AMERICA RETIRES.
BUT CAN IT AFFORD TO?

CHAPTER ONE

THE SHAKING OF THE FOUNDATIONS: RETIREMENT AT A CRITICAL CROSSROADS

The main purpose of this book is to get you to think differently about retirement, to get you to realize that the old rules no longer apply, since trends beyond your control are reshaping retirement right now. This is the first crisis of meaning in the history of the U.S. retirement system. Historic social changes have swept retirement up into an unprecedented state of flux. Increased life expectancy, the sheer size of the baby boom generation that is just now entering retirement, and the replacement of pensions with 401(K)-type plans are the three big blows to the old retirement, the three irreversible shifts that are shaking retirement at its foundations.

LONGEVITY IS KILLING US

It wasn't that long ago that the average retirement lasted no more than 10 years. For the new generation, 10 years marks the *first stage* of a retirement that can easily last 30 years or more. Naturally, longer lives mean increased risk of outliving retirement savings.

What is the impact of this huge new variable on the retirement equation? The first reaction is to state the obvious: in order to prevent poverty, we will be working longer. Beyond postponing retirement, however, the question that still needs answering is, how can you offset the risks that the new longevity poses to your retirement, once you decide to begin it?

Taking care not to outlive retirement savings used to mean simply planning ahead and investing part of your savings to make sure your dollars are not eaten away by inflation. In the retirement equation of earlier generations, you could balance the risk of living through one market crash with the security of relying on Social Security to see you through the rough patch. If you were unlucky enough to be hit by a serious downturn in retirement, the chances of it ever happening again were minuscule. More importantly, retirees knew that they could always rely on that check in the mail from the government.

The danger that longevity poses is that it increases the number of times your retirement portfolio gets exposed to market crashes. Market cycles of booms and crashes do not come around every couple of years, so a ten-year retirement could be lived without obsessing about their impact. What happens when suddenly the vast majority of retirees live through four or six market cycles? Should it change the way you prepare for and react to the inevitable downturn in the market? And if so, how?

Talking heads continue to argue over whether Social Security will go broke, what it will take to save it, how to adjust it, whether we should revamp it, and so on. As important as these debates are, I will not be weighing in on any one specific issue or taking sides with any of the commentators or public policy makers. Instead, consider the following question that cuts to the chase: Does anyone under 55 really believe that they will always be able to count on Social Security as a hedge against bad investment decisions? Why not? What has happened to explain this loss of faith?

THE NEW GENERATION

No one can think about the status of Social Security for more than five minutes without noticing the huge demographic bulge, the "pig in the python,"[1] that the baby boom generation represents. The 79 million baby boomers who began retiring in 2006 are almost twice the size of the generation before them *and* after them. The boomers really stick out. It would be bad enough if the boomers were entering retirement with the same life expectancy and the same savings rates as their parents. But it's worse than that. It would be bad enough if the boomers were having the same number of children as their parents. But it's worse than that. Life expectancy has shot up, birth rates have plummeted and, until very recently, savings rates were at nearly negative levels.

"Baby boom generation" is a term that refers to the 79 million Americans born between 1945 and 1964. The "New Generation" mentioned in the title refers loosely to the baby boomers, without fussing too much over the precise demarcations and borders between generations and cohorts within them. To suggest that the redefinition undertaken here is specific only to one generation as narrowly defined would understate the magnitude of the changes that we are witnessing and the challenges they pose.

Retirement is undergoing a seismic shift. The word *seismic* comes from the Greek *seismos*, which translates to "earthquake," and stems from the word *seien*, which means "to shake." The solutions we find as we redefine retirement, as the situation on the ground forces us to, will provide a new template—a timely and relevant framework—for understanding retirement for generations to come. Nevertheless, thinking about the baby boomers as a cultural group with similar behaviors and expectations is a great way to gain insight into the depth of the current crisis.

It is striking for instance, that the baby boomers were the only generation to be named after their parents' high fertility rates. If Social Security had a passing grade when the huge generation of boomers was contributing to it, while a relatively small generation was taking from it, what shape will it be in as demographics reverse this give and take relationship, as they will do, steadily, with no sign of letting up? Members of the largest generation ever to become eligible for Social Security share two behavioral traits that, like the three big social trends, have already cast the die for their future retirement struggles.

Boomers saved much less than the generation before them and had far fewer children. Lower birth rates mean a smaller pool of retirement savings will have to be replenished with a thinner income stream from Social Security.

Yet another first that sets the boomer generation apart from all other generations is how it sought a cure from retirement anxiety through investing in mutual funds. Now that the era of exuberant enthusiasm in the market has ended, we see clearly how bad investment decisions can have catastrophic consequences for our lifestyle in retirement. And as nice as they may sound to a generation living through the worst economy since the Great Depression, guaranteed pension plans are about as common today as TVs built into cabinets. Which brings us to another foundational change facing the new generation.

BRAVE NEW WORLD, THAT HAS NO PENSIONS IN IT

The boomers are the first generation to face the demise of the old pension plan and the total domination of 401(k)-type plans. Now, individuals must cope with a new range of risks that have proliferated as traditional pensions (defined *benefit* plans) have been crushed under the wave of 401(k) plans (defined *contribution* plans). During the time of the 401(k) takeover—from the mid 1980s up to 2000, faith in the stock market made exposure to it seem like gaining access to an unending income stream. The decimation of 401(k)s in 2008/09 offers a window for looking out to the future of retirement.

As we will see, the trouble is that the basic components of retirement that made it work in the past are now in disarray, while changes in retirement benefits have transferred the risk away from employers and onto the shoulders of individuals. Market booms and busts will always be with us, but the crisis facing us today is a momentous event.

A NEW DEFINITION FOR A NEW LANDSCAPE

It has never been more important to understand all the risks involved, both old and new, and to think more pragmatically about the meaning of retirement and the best methods for generating as many reliable income streams as possible. So this book sets out to define retirement, to describe it as-is, and then to redefine it, to lay out moves that can be made right now, to prepare to live a life of freedom in the later stages of your life. In this way, the book is an invitation to devote a few hours to concentrating on the wide array of elements and aspects of retirement, bits and pieces of which we all see, hear, and comment on throughout the day, as we watch the news, read the papers, and share our thoughts with our loved ones, friends, colleagues, and neighbors.

Even in an environment untouched by radical market upheaval—an environment, that is, very different from our own—retirement in America would still be facing the same grave threats of internal weakness and misconceptions regarding the risk involved in building a retirement plan around enthusiasm for the stock market. It is as if a whole generation, confident in the knowledge of the directions they have received, pressed on to their destination, only to discover that neither the directions nor their ability to follow them were as black and white as they had supposed. Today, the boomer generation has pulled over to the side of the road to get its bearings—to say, "Wait a minute, this doesn't look right." This book is intended as a resource for anyone who has pulled off the road in this way, to pause and make sure the directions are correct, to see whether they have been looking at the map upside down, and to take action to get back on track and reach their destination.

WHAT MAKES FOR A USEFUL REDEFINITION OF RETIREMENT?

This book identifies the broken parts of the system and, most importantly, provides a strategy for individuals who want to understand and avoid the various hazards of an increasingly risky retirement system. As traditional and assumed sources of retirement income continue to dry up, the primary challenge is to devise and discover alternatives that will last. A useful redefinition of retirement will successfully dispel the myth that investing is always safe and, as long as you stay invested, no matter what the circumstances, you will come out ahead.

Redefining retirement means taking a fresh look at all the assets to which individuals have access, and thinking in new ways about how to put those assets to work to generate lasting income. So the over-arching question that the book poses is how to make sense of all these changes within the context of a concrete plan that prepares you for a secure retirement, however long it lasts.

You can tell by the size of this book that it is not intended as an academic contribution to history of thought on retirement in America. But then neither is it a cookie cutter "how to" book. It's hard to see how any such book would be worth the time it took to read it. Oversimplifications and clichés are part of the problem, part of what must be swept away before we can arrive at a practical definition of retirement that can provide solutions to individuals in the real world. My intention here is to provide a simple guide for individuals who want to understand the new retirement as it relates to them. There is no one-size-fits-all list of rules that can get you from here to there, but there are principles. For instance:

- Understand the nature of the risks you are taking

- Demand transparency
- Beware of hidden fees
- Remember we will all be living a lot longer
- Don't rely on the government to provide you with retirement security
- Don't chase trends
- Take simple steps to make your employer's retirement plan works for you and not against you
- Stay away from actively traded mutual funds
- Explore all the assets at your disposal
- Remember that a market crash at the wrong time can wipe out a portfolio of stocks

This book presents these principles within an overview of the nexus of systems, institutions, demographics, trends, behavioral choices, investment products and styles, portfolio construction, scams and scandals that make up the cultural institution of retirement in America. Each area of the terrain covered contains enough data and debate to fill a book itself. All I have endeavored to do in these pages is present a series of snapshots from a vast landscape. The first part of redefining retirement examines the current conditions and underlying trends that have lead to the crisis, in order to understand and avoid the big mistakes while navigating retirement as it stands today. Then, in Part Two, we will examine some new directions in the philosophy of investing, and review the clash of conventional thinking about investing for retirement and the new realities.

CHAPTER TWO

TICKING TIME BOMBS BETWEEN THE FOLDS OF RETIREMENT

Retirement is practically brand new. Before the 1950s, there was not much of a concept of retirement to speak of, and the freedom to stop working while you were still able bodied was a benefit of acquiring great wealth, not planning for retirement. By 1960, retirement had become a nationwide employee benefit, with half of private sector employees and all public sector employees covered by a pension plan.[2] From its beginnings in 1950 to the present day, the idea of a planned retirement has been anchored by the notion of the three-legged retirement stool. You can still find the three-legged stool idea in brochures for consumers, textbooks, and training manuals for financial advisers.

RETIREMENT USED TO BE LIKE A THREE-LEGGED STOOL

The three-legged stool refers to the three traditional sources of retirement income: Social Security, personal savings, and pension plans. Its beauty is its simplicity. Conventional wisdom holds that the three-legged retirement stool should be built like this: 15%-25% of retirement income should come from Social Security, 0%-60% from a pension plan, and any gap between the two should be filled by private savings—the third leg. Did the concept of the three-legged stool work?

Did it ever. Financially secure retirement time expanded nationally right through the early-1950s to the mid-1970s, when people born around 1911 began retiring. This age group entered retirement at a time when Social Security benefits increased rapidly, and secure company-provided pension plans were spreading like wildfire.[3] The three-legged stool is a great metaphor for what this age group had to do to retire. When you hear the word "stool" you automatically understand that a good sturdy stool depends on its three legs being balanced right. And it makes it easy to remember the three income streams to focus on in order to plan for retirement. Pensions came from your company, Social Security from the government, and savings from you.

After the mid-1970s, however, the ground started shifting in all directions. Retirement time actually started going down in the mid-1980s for the first time ever. Over the same time period, the three big blows to the old retirement—the huge boomer generation, longevity, and 401(k)-type retirement plans—were just gathering strength. Today, they dominate.

THE 3 BLOWS AGAINST THE
THREE–LEGGED RETIREMENT STOOL

The first blow: The aging boomers

Currently, boomers represent over 27% of the American population and 47% of all households.[4] As they continue to retire over the next 20 years, the boomers will become dependent on Social Security, retirement plans, and any accumulated assets. The demographic "pig in the python" will turn the relationship between Social Security recipients and contributors upside down.

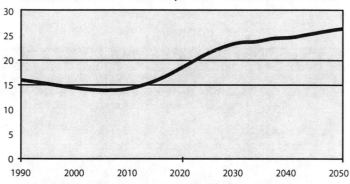

Boomers Enter Retirement Years:

Number of Persons 65+ Years Old per 100 Persons 18 to 65 Years Old

Source: *Age Power: How the 21st Century Will Be Ruled by the New Old*, 1999, Ken Dychtwald, Ph.D.

Figure 1

In 2006, the first members of the largest generation in American history turned 60. Also in 2006, the Social Security taxes that went directly to funding the demand for payouts reached 86%. Up to now, this largest of all generations has been funding the Social Security of their parents' generation, all the while assuming that their retirement will be smoother, more luxurious, and longer lasting than their parents. Unfortunately, the only one of these assumptions that connects to the facts is the last one, as science and statistics tell us that life expectancy rates are shooting upward.

Blow #2: Living longer, much longer

With improvements in healthcare, nutrition and technology, life expectancy has almost doubled over the past century. As figure 2 shows, for a 65-year-old couple today, there is a 63% chance that one will reach the age of 90.[5]

Longevity

Probability of living from age 65 to...			
Age	Male	Female	Probability of One Spouse Living
70	93%	96%	99%
75	84%	90%	98%
80	71%	81%	94%
85	53%	65%	83%
90	33%	44%	63%
95	16%	23%	36%

Source: "Annuity 2000 Mortality Table," Society of Actuaries
Figure 2

The boomers' significant increase in life expectancy unleashes levels of risk that the world has never seen before. Now the danger of outliving your assets comes into play in every retirement decision. In addition to worrying about whether inflation is eating away at their savings in retirement, boomers must also face the prospect of preserving their investment portfolios through multiple market crashes.

Blow #3: The Death of Pensions

For the first time, the majority of Fortune 100 companies now offer new salaried employees only a 401(k)-type plan. This is up from 46% at the end of 2007. And even among the 45 companies that offer a traditional pension, 23 had a hybrid plan that combines elements of a 401(k). We have entered a whole new world for retirement benefits. You may be one of the millions of Americans who began your career with a traditional pension pan only to have it switched over to a 401(k) plan. Perhaps you are one of the few who still has a traditional pension. If so, you can bet your employer is under pressure to eliminate it and follow the 401(k) trend.

Boomers with pension plans have counted on monthly checks at the end of their career, but more employers are ending their plans or stopping future benefits. The number of pension plans in the U.S. peaked at 175,000 in 1983, and has since declined to less than 25,000. Roughly 30% of the remaining pension programs plan to close very soon.[6] Those at greatest risk include boomers in their late 40s and early

50s, who are still at least a decade from retirement but too old to save enough to make up the difference. The traditional company-owned pension that provides income until the day you die is itself all but dead.

Under the new 401(k)-type plans, the amount of income you collect after retirement and how long you continue to receive are unknown. Nothing is guaranteed. In this way, the risk of retirement has been shifted away from the employer and placed upon the shoulders of the individual. Boomers will be the first generation to rely on 401(k) plans exclusively for their retirement savings. It's a big burden for them to carry, as the market meltdown of 2008/09 made all too clear.

There are those who are quick to remind us that, taken from a historical perspective, the loss of 401(k) savings, though painful, is a small event in an isolated area and is therefore not particularly noteworthy. Even if we do, for the sake of argument, agree that the evaporation of $2 trillion in 401(k) savings in 2008/09 was an isolated incident, the event still stands as the first tangible warning of the larger developing problem—it shows how we are gradually losing our grip on retirement.

THE COLLAPSE OF RETIREMENT INCOME AND THE DEATH OF THE THREE-LEGGED STOOL

The trouble is that too much easy talk about retirement's

three-legged stool can lull you into a false sense of security, and make you complacent about the new threats that current events have put in your way. By identifying three revenue sources, the model suggests two false and potentially devastating propositions:

- That the three sources are all reliable
- That they are all we have

As we shall see, they're not, not by a long shot.

The three-legged stool has become a one-legged stool— at best; nevertheless, many policy makers, financial advisers, 401(k) providers, and financial marketers continue to speak in terms of the old model as if it were as relevant today as it was 50 years ago. Fifty years ago Social Security had solid funding. Fifty years ago good careers included guaranteed pensions. Fifty years ago individuals entered retirement having saved a goodly portion of what they earned. Over the past three decades, each of these sources of income has been in speedy retreat.

In spite of these sobering facts, the boomer generation has been quite optimistic about retirement—right up to the great recession of 2009. But then, boomers are a very optimistic bunch. Studies of boomer behavioral traits have determined that optimism is one of the main attitudes shared by members of this generation.[7] Another unique feature of the boomers is that they tend to think of themselves as a special generation, very different from those that had come before them. As we shall have time to explore in chapter two, boomer optimism and arrogance go a long way in explaining why retirement problems are not more at the forefront of national debate. Right now, it will be useful to see boomer optimism at work in attitudes toward retirement generally. As it turns out, the great recession has provided an interesting twist that no one predicted.

THE TYPICAL BOOMER RESPONSE:
"IT CAN'T HAPPEN TO ME."

In 1998, it was reported boomers tended to avoid discussions and planning for their demise and avoided much long term planning.[8] However, some signs of dialogue on how to manage aging and retirement issues began shortly after that time.[9] As late as 2007, commentators were arguing that boomers were in a state of denial regarding their own aging and death and leaving an undue economic burden on their children for their retirement and care.[10]

In 2006, 68% of employees were confident that they would have a comfortable retirement.[11] The same survey taken in 2009 shows confidence swinging from a majority to a minority position, with only 41% of respondents saying they are somewhat confident that they will have enough money to retire, and a small group of optimists 13%, saying they are very confident.[12]

Figure 3 sketches a dismal picture of the outlook for today's retirees. Among retirees, only 20%—versus 41% in

2007—are very confident of being able to afford a financially secure retirement. Just 25% say they expect to have enough to pay for medical expenses, down from 41% in 2007. And only 34% are optimistic about covering their basic expenses, compared with 48% two years ago. Clearly, the gap between the boomers' vision of retirement and the reality of retired life has narrowed more than it would have, had the financial crisis of 2009 never occurred.

Losing Faith

Only 13% of workers are very confident that they will have enough for a comfortable retirement - down sharply from just two years ago:

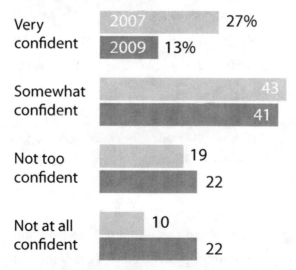

Source: *Life and Death Planning for Retirement Benefits*, 2002, Natalie Choate
Figure 3

The big question is whether the new willingness to acknowledge that there is a crisis in retirement will fade—

whether the experience of a genuine market crash will continue to teach its very important message, namely, that investing in the stock market can be a very risky proposition. If the great recession of 2008/09 has a silver lining, it will be that it made us realize that our retirement plans are not indestructible, that the devastating losses that splashed across the headlines were tragedies that could happen to any one of us.

THE DAY THE RULES OF RETIREMENT CHANGED

It's Friday, September 21, 2008, and these are the morning headlines. "ALMOST ARMAGEDDON: MARKETS WERE 500 TRADES FROM A MELTDOWN." The first two sentences of the page one article give the gist of what just happened:

> The market was 500 trades away from Armageddon on Thursday, traders inside two large custodial banks tell The Post.

> Had the Treasury and Fed not quickly stepped into the fray that morning with a quick $105 billion injection of liquidity, the Dow could have collapsed.[13]

It looks as if the stock market will meltdown in front of your eyes. What would unfold over the next year would be a historic event: The great wealth destruction of 2009. It meant the evaporation of over two trillion dollars in retirement savings. The unprecedented losses hit those closest to retirement hardest. Many who were about to retire gave up their plans, hoped to stay working, started looking for new work. Retirement was no longer an option. Not for now. Others, to whom retirement was a new luxury, had to get back to work. Fast.

Of course, Armageddon never came. Another headline from another day could just as well have been chosen to open this discussion. The point would be the same: The hard times that descended in 2008 caused not only hardship and suffering, but also forced a confrontation. Just as the largest generation of retirees in history began entering the system, the very idea of retirement was suddenly up in the air.

The economic crash of 2009 crystallized the pressures and risks that had been building up over the past two decades. The crash was a wake up call to all aging boomers, as well as younger generations, that retirement is no way a given. It's not something that just happens. The question is whether the boomers will get their wake up calls on time, and see the need to understand retirement, to see how it is changing, so that they can redefine it for themselves, in a way that applies directly to their personal goals.

TOSSING THE THREE-LEGGED RETIREMENT
STOOL INTO THE DUST BIN OF HISTORY

In order to get a handle on retirement in the modern world, it is important to think of it not so much as a static stool whose balance requires that its three legs all be the same size, but rather as a scaffolding with multiple modules, built to react to the storms that are bound to come and go over the course of two or three decade-long retirement.

Today, many of us become our own worst enemies as we fail to save and choose to depend on credit. Even for those of us for whom this is not the case, the pension system is in free fall, Social Security limps along with no clear program to insure its long-term solvency, and medical costs continue to skyrocket. With the old arteries drying up, asset allocation planning becomes the only thing the individual can depend on to provide a secure retirement.

In order to make up for the depletion of revenue streams, we have to explore new income sources and expand the basic range of asset classes we have to work with. For instance, insurance solutions are just now taking shape in response to retirement's malaise. Portfolio design has been reinvented in our time, and its benefits are just beginning to be made available to the individual investor. Assets from beyond the three traditional categories of stocks, bonds, and cash are being quantified with new precision and used to create better diversification. We will have time to discuss some of these smart investment solutions in Part Two. For now we would do best to continue to observe the connection between boomer optimism and the inclination to deny that there is any real problem with retirement.

In the next chapter we move from demographic trends to the boomers' behavioral traits. These are behaviors that most members of a generation hold in common. Two boomer traits in particular—low birth rates and low saving rates—have shaped the new generations' retirement prospects just as much as the three big trends discussed above.

CHAPTER THREE

FROM GREATEST GENERATION TO THE GENERATION OF GREATEST UNCERTAINTY

The new generation's main contribution to the collapse of retirement income is its low savings rates and low birth rates. Boomers simply stopped saving what they earned. The odd thing is that it hasn't seemed to affect their optimistic outlook about the prospects of their own retirement. Not until very recently anyway. For the first time ever, boomers are expressing real anxiety about retirement. The great recession of 2008/09 has cracked the armor of boomer optimism, and for the first time, the new generation has grown pessimistic about retirement. The new generation has also started, again for the first time, to increase its savings rates.

Will these shifts in boomer attitudes and behavior last, or will savings revert back to their negative rates? Will the younger cohorts within the boomer generation take an active interest in retirement? Or will good news and better times lull boomers back into a lazy optimism about life in retirement? This chapter considers the impact of the boomers' choices and outlooks on the retirement system they have just begun to enter. The story starts with the astonishing disappearance of boomer savings rates.

BOOMERS REJECT THE PRACTICE OF SAVING

If you still think that the three-legged stool might be useful to understand retirement for the new generation, consider the story of boomer savings rates told in figure 4.

The second leg of the old three-legged retirement stool, you will remember, was personal savings. It was based on the simple economic idea of life-cycle consumption. The idea was that an individual saves little as a young adult, a lot in his middle ages, and not at all when he retires. The key was that in your middle ages, you filled up the second leg of the retirement stool. You saved what you earned when those earnings were at their peak. For the boomers' parents, everything fit together well, with their household savings rate rising from below 15% in their early 20s to about 30% in their late 40s.[14]

Boomer Saving Rates Have Not Peaked during Prime Earning Years Like Previous Generations

Saving rate by cohort, household balance sheet measure
% of disposable income

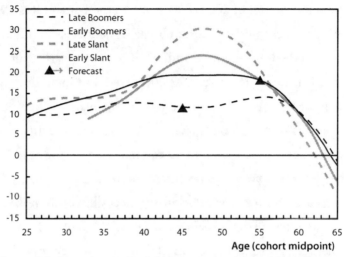

Source: *Talkin' 'bout my generation: the economic impact of aging U.S. baby boomers,* 2008, McKinsey Global Institute

Figure 4

But that pattern—essential to the very idea of a three-legged retirement stool—gets laid to waste by the baby boom generation. Notice that the pattern is almost absent for early boomers, those born 1945 to 1954; their saving rate tops out about 20%; and it's completely absent for late boomers, those born 1955 to 1964, whose saving rate so far has remained stuck at around 10%.

The study that generated the data in figure 4, *Talkin' 'bout my generation: The economic impact of aging U.S. Baby Boomers,* shows that "the Boomers' missing savings peak accounts for most of the collapse in the U.S. household saving rate from its peak of over 10 percent in the mid-1980s to around 2 percent today."[15]

The national savings rate averaged 0.9% of after-tax income in September 2007 (according to the Federal Reserve Board). According to the Employee Benefit Research Institute's 2008 Retirement Confidence Survey, nearly half of Americans have less than $25,000 saved, not including the value of their homes or their retirement plans. When one cupboard starts to look bare, it's natural to turn and flip open the one next to it, to see if you can make up for the scarcity. Realizing that you have nothing in personal savings can fix your attention on Social Security. After all, you have been paying into it all these years. So what will be waiting for you? To brace yourself, keep in mind that the boomers have had significantly fewer children than their parents. The boomers are 79 million strong; the next generation is made up of a mere 31 million. So progressively smaller generations are just now being asked to support boomers' unfunded benefits, along with their own healthcare and retirement needs. These numbers simply do not add up.

THE NEW IRRELEVANCE OF SOCIAL SECURITY

Today, the funding for Social Security and Medicare is so under-financed and actuarially shaky that you cannot be certain those programs will exist at all by the time you're eligible for them. The new generation that is now working will receive a much lower rate of return on their Social Security contributions than their parents. Though the rates of returns are very low across the board for the boomers, they are worst for those whose contributions were highest. Figure 5 illustrates this Social Security "catch 22", where the more you put into the system, the less you recoup in old age.

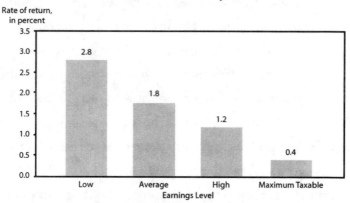

Return on Social Security Contributions

Source: Congressional Budget Office

Figure 5

The payroll tax revenue that finances Social Security benefits for nearly 51 million retirees and other recipients continues to fall, according to a report from the Congressional Budget Office. As a result, the trust fund's annual surplus was forecast to all but vanish by 2010—a decade ahead of schedule. Prior to the publishing of this report, the Social Security Administration forecasts predicted the Social Security Trust Fund would be bankrupt by 2020. This kind of data leads logically to debates over the sustainability of Social Security.

Some experts see the data and conclude that Social Security is effectively bankrupt already. Others argue that the death of Social Security has been greatly exaggerated. By all means, acquaint yourself with these discussions and develop your own views on the various opinions and policy proposals. Our mission in this compact book is not so much to weigh in on these broader issues as to say: Wait. Let's be clear that retirement income has collapsed here. The money will not be there, so you cannot assume you can count on it when you most need it. Instead of counting on Social Security to take up the slack for the absence of savings, wouldn't it make more sense to figure out how to provide your own Self Security? After all, what is the mandate of Social Security if not to provide the minimum you need to live forever.

Forget about the three-legged retirement stool. Instead, consider the utility of the retirement scaffolding framework. The solution is to add a new module to your retirement scaffolding—to figure out the minimum you would need in retirement, the bare minimum, then set out a strategy for obtaining it and locking it in. Figure it out. Write it down. Then connect the Self Security module to the rest of the scaffold. Self Security would cover guaranteed retirement income. Beware of the hurdles. Know yourself. Take advantage of the vast amount of research that has been done on the boomer generation, and stay mindful of the boomer tendency to look at retirement through rose-colored glasses.

BOOMER OPTIMISM AND BOOMER DENIAL

The boomers have always been associated with privilege, as many grew up in a time of great affluence. As a group, they are the healthiest and wealthiest generation in history, and among the first to grow up genuinely expecting the world to improve with time. It should come as no surprise that their views on retirement reflect their exceptionally optimistic predisposition.

A survey whose topic overlaps with the title of this book provides a great example of the problem. The main question in the survey was:

How would you redefine retirement? It is fair to speculate that the generation before the boomers would have assumed the survey was asking about how to increase your retirement savings, or decrease your retirement spending?

The question really was put to boomers, who responded by talking about lifestyle choices, healthy activities, travel, blending in some part-time work and perhaps volunteering. In other words, the survey provoked responses that sought to make retirement even more perfect.

Just four years before the crash of 2009, in 2005, boomers worried more about how to spend their time in retirement than whether they would have enough money to remain independent. Pre-market crash, redefining retirement had more to do with getting rid of stereotypes of retirees as coping with old age and imagining the time more as an opportunity to carry on a young adult lifestyle after leaving one's career. As long as the stock market continued to climb, the shifting meaning of retirement did not seem to matter much. The Social Security and personal savings that earlier generations relied on no longer seemed relevant, now that America had a sophisticated investor class that would only continue to prosper as a result of their superior education and knowledge.

Commenting on *The New Retirement Survey* from 2005, Ken Dychtwald, co-sponsor of the study said: "It appears that boomer men and women are generally optimistic, innovative and hopeful—and they're definitely gearing up for a new model of retirement. We asked boomers for their hopes, fears and thoughts about retirement and what we got was the systematic dismantling of all of our preconceptions about the future, for not only this generation, but for nearly all of society's institutions."[16]

This attitude to retirement as an old institution that had to be reinvigorated with the new blood of the boomers was part of a decade-long trend of growing optimism. In every query, boomers in this 2005 survey expressed more optimism than they did five years prior. For instance, baby boomers were far more likely in 2005 than in 2000 to describe themselves as knowledgeable about and favorably predisposed toward Social Security. Boomers were also more confident that Medicare would be available when they reach age 65.

As recently as 2006, new retirees expected to live more luxuriously than previous generations. According to the 2006 survey, boomers approaching retirement expected to escalate their lifestyles in retirement. In hindsight, the optimism expressed by boomers sounds like the out of touch musings of a generation in denial. The gap between the old optimism and the current reality raises some fundamental questions:

- How did the most well educated generation in the history of the planet arrive at a view of retirement so detached from reality?
- Now that the great financial crisis of 2008/09 has awakened the boomers from their retirement daydreams, how can the reality of their circumstances be measured?

In fact, the three-legged retirement stool metaphor applies only secondarily to the current retiring generation. Its primary application is to the generation that preceded it, what Tom Brokaw famously coined "the greatest generation." In addition to benefiting from the institutional strength mentioned above, the greatest generation also benefited in retirement from what it did not have. That is, it did not have easy credit. It did not have a government and financial industry pushing it away from pensions and into the stock market, and it did not have a birth rate in steep decline. Nor was life expectancy for the prior generation climbing exponentially. Breaking with the old three-legged stool metaphor is important. Failure to do so is indicative of the boomer inclination to cling to unrealistic dreams.

EASY PREY

Overconfidence and unrealistic expectations have made the new generation easy prey to those who would sell the idea that we are smart enough to invest in ways that beat the market—so we don't have to worry about Social Security or personal savings, or the details of our retirement plans, as long as we keep contributing. There is no doubt that the old definition, with its myths and easy answers, will continue to survive. For its part, the financial industry did everything in its power to suggest that baby boomers were entitled to a carefree retirement on a pillow of income from their portfolios.

For three decades, a narrative of retirement images has poured out from televisions and PCs.

- Retired beautiful people on day-long walks along the seaside
- Sunshine, loved ones, friends and family in exotic locals
- Tennis in the afternoon
- Dining alfresco with neighbors in the evening

In this world, the retirees are not like any that have come before: everyone is active, healthy, smart, energetic, curious, and free. Sailing is common; worry about the future, a thing of the past, as enlightened baby boomers draw from unlimited income from participation in the ever-expanding stock market.

BOOMER CONVERSION?

The bleak landscape at the threshold of retirement does not fit with the baby boomers' conception of themselves, their conception of what they have worked for, what they should have now, or what they should expect to have in the future. After all, the boomers oversaw countless huge leaps in technology and computerized information systems; they witnessed precision and predictability in science and social sciences advance exponentially, bringing increases in quality of life, curing diseases, and solving a variety of poverty-related social ills.

By early 2009, in less than one year, market contractions made hash of the retirement utopia that the financial industry spent over a decade marketing to the public. Today's mandate is a stern either/or: either redefine retirement or continue to suffer from exposure to the ills of a broken system. Boomers are beginning to wake up to reality.

According to the sponsor of the 2009 survey, Mr. Van-Derhei, retirees have begun to realize that there is "a huge gap between what people think it's going to take to retire comfortably and what it actually takes." Many people will be forced to settle for a "much lower standard of living in retirement than what they had hoped for," he says.

And here we see one reason why getting retirement right requires redefinition. The retirement utopianism pumped out through the marketing wings of our financial institutions carried along with it a subtle yet unchanging message. The myth is this: All you need to depend on for your retirement are your investments in the markets. It is in this context that the economist Nassim Taleb, author of *The Black Swan*, talked about what the great recession of 2009 can teach us about retirement: "We should learn not to use markets as storehouses of value: they do not harbor the certainties that normal citizens require. Citizens should experience anxiety about their own businesses (which they control), not their investments (which they do not control)." If retirement security is not all about betting on the stock market to make all things right, what is it?

THE BOOMER SENSE OF ENTITLEMENT

It is not difficult to imagine a baby boomer at age 50 in 2003 feeling satisfied in the knowledge that his generation was the first to witness the rise of the investor class. With steady market gains feeding confidence in their investing prowess, boomers could let the pending insolvency of Social Security and the significance of paltry personal savings pass through one ear and out the other. Returns from modern mutual funds would be the new path to retirement security.

After all, on the face of it, the old assumption seems so

sensible: the progress and advances that materialized during the boomer generation should also take place at the stage of retirement. Why shouldn't advances in living standards, infant mortality, death and disease, and employment opportunities, (to name only a few of the cultural, economic, and scientific achievements witnessed and enjoyed by the boomer generation) translate into a systematic and tranquil transformation from working life to retired life? This attitude of entitlement among boomers is surely part of the explanation as to how the three-legged stool of retirement could become so shaky without any outcry.

The thought continues: If you play by the rules, don't take unreasonable chances, stay gainfully employed, take advantage of investment vehicles at your disposal, then your retirement will be better than earlier generations. Boomer retirements and retirement readiness should trend toward a quality and security unmatched by earlier generations. Unfortunately, the data shows trend lines headed in precisely the opposite direction.

NEW RULES FOR COPING WITH NEW UNCERTAINTY

Needing or desiring to work longer doesn't make it so. We know that 25% of boomers say they plan to postpone retirement. (The age at which workers say they plan to retire has crept up from a median of 62 in 1991 to 65 since 2004.) However, almost half of current retirees say they left the work force sooner than expected, frequently because of health problems or downsizings. Moreover, while the survey has consistently found that about two-thirds of workers plan to work after retiring, fewer than 35% of current retirees say they have actually held down jobs at some point during retirement.

Perhaps your desire to work longer as a way of shoring up against the risks of your longer life will be possible. How much of a difference will it make? What is your plan B, if working longer turns out not to be an option? You will have to think creatively about the mix of revenue streams you have or would like to have by the time you retire, whenever that turns out to actually happen. The investment industry will tell you that stocks are supposed to protect you from the ravages of inflation. And since stocks tend to outpace most investments over long periods of time, your savings will do all right in the end. The operative phrase in that last sentence is "tend to." In fact, there is a new study[17] that echoes the worries that many investors developed during the course of the great recession. The report says that holding stocks over long periods of time may be riskier than previously thought. Robert F. Stambaugh, a finance professor at the Wharton School at the University of Pennsylvania and a co-author of the report, said most investment research only accounted for the risk of short-term market swings around the stock market's average gain over time. It doesn't factor in the fact that the average itself is subject to change.

Counting on stocks to hedge against outliving your money in a long retirement could make sense, if you have accumulated enough wealth to withstand another extreme downturn without being utterly devastated. But what if a downturn wiped you out? It may be in your best interest to design a module for an immediate fixed annuity in order to guarantee that you'll be able to cover your basic expenses.

The annuity pays you a stream of income until you die. That's not to say that building an annuity module would safeguard you from uncertainty altogether. What if the company that provided you with the annuity goes bust? Perhaps it would be best to take out several small such annuities so that if one goes down, you will still have the others. Here again, we run up against the limits of the retirement stool for the new generation. The way we conceive of retirement must accommodate the array of uncertainties that the modern world presents.

The retirement scaffolding model takes into account hard-headed assessments of what must be done to retire with peace and security.

CHAPTER FOUR

ACTIVELY MANAGED MUTUAL FUNDS ARE POISONING YOUR RETIREMENT

Actively managed mutual funds poison everything, and if your retirement planning affords them a central role, they could poison it as well. Is this the same as saying that there is no such thing as an actively managed mutual fund that is worth its cost? No. They do exist. The problem is that it is all but impossible to say where they are until it is too late to benefit from them. This is more than an opinion based on experience; it is a conclusion to be drawn by anyone taking a level-headed look at the historical data.

There are over 7,000 mutual funds from which to choose. Of these, many fail to do as well as the stock market itself. This bleak statistic has held true almost universally over the past four decades. It has never been refuted or even seriously debated. That is, when the market is up for the year, many actively managed mutual funds are not up as much; when the market is down, these same funds are down even more. Alright then, you may say, what we are after then are the few funds that are excluded from the pack of under-performers. There are two reasons this response, though apparently sensible enough, is completely misguided.

CAN ANYONE PICK A WINNING MUTUAL FUND MONEY MANAGER?

The actively traded funds in the small category of non-losers include those who broke even and, in rare cases, did better than the market *before* fees, additional costs, and taxes. Before you can assess the value of these funds, it is imperative to draw the distinction between *investment* success and *investor* success. A mutual fund may be able to say it has done as well as the market. But that proposition does not speak to the success of the individual invested in the fund. Returns for the fund itself and returns for the individual investor are always two different figures. Guess which number is usually lower.

The money manager of the mutual fund gets paid to play, while the investor has to pay to play. Once they are all figured in, the costs of being a shareholder in the "winning" mutual fund almost always cancel out the gains about which everyone is so happy and vocal.

True, some actively managed mutual funds have proven that they could run through the gauntlet of costs and still deliver added value to the individual investor. It is difficult to come up with a definitive number here, because so many costs to the investor are not always apparent and taxes fluctuate, which brings us to the second problem with picking winning actively managed mutual funds.

With so many mutual funds doing worse than the market, what are the chances of a particular money manager having a truly winning fund? More importantly, what are the chances of you or your investment advisor picking the winning fund ahead of time? The odds are not in your favor. Yet this is precisely the bad bet that every shareholder in an actively managed mutual fund makes—year after year. Making matters worse, the data makes it clear that the larger the mutual fund gets—that is, the more assets it gathers from individuals—the worse it performs. So the *investor surge* into a mutual fund with impressive gains seals the fund's fate as a future under-performer.

How can this be? Consider a survey with consistently odd results. In his landmark book, *Irrational Exuberance,*18 Robert Schiller, a Yale economist, asked investors two simple questions. First, do they believe that they or their advisors or brokers, can achieve long-term financial benefit by selecting individual stocks? The answer was a resounding "no." Second question: Do they believe that they or their advisors can provide long-term financial benefit by selecting actively managed mutual funds? As many who said no to the first question said yes to the second. What to make of this odd belief that we have the capacity to pick mutual funds but not individual stocks?

"There must be a way to pick the right actively managed mutual fund, otherwise we've all had it." Perhaps this suspension of suspicion arises from the assumption that there is no other way to invest for the long-term. Happily, that assumption is just flat wrong. (More on this at the end of the chapter.) Before anything else—before the additional costs, the structural flaws, the misleading advertising, the potential for manipulation of results—it is this fundamental dilemma at the heart of mutual fund investing, the inability to pick the winners, that throws the viability of mutual fund investing into question. For example, consider the following "advice" on choosing a mutual fund offered by a Wall Street Journal-sponsored investment education website:

> **❝** Which fund or funds out of the 7000 plus should you pick? *The most important thing to look for when evaluating a fund is its performance record.* By this I don't mean just go buy the best- performing funds of the moment. Instead, look for consistent winners, ones that had few, if any, down years, ones that held up well in bear markets, ones that had double digit gains consistently. Historically, the hottest funds of one year usually did poorly for the following years.

And then the concluding sentence of the paragraph reads:

> " Past performance record is *probably* the best
>   indicator for long-term performance.[19]

Probably? Didn't the advice begin by saying that it is the *most important thing*? The honesty of the above paragraph can only leave an investor scratching his—or her—head.

Very few of the top 100 money managers stay in that category the next year; top performance in one year fails to predict a manager's ability to beat the market the next year. The only thing the data suggests is that if a manager has beaten the market this year, the market is likely to beat him next year. From 1997 to 2007 for instance, there is only a 7% repeat success rate. So the most rational decision, based on the evidence, would be to pick next year's winner from this year's losers. Facts like these led the Securities and Exchange Commission to mandate that every piece of mutual fund sales literature contain the following warning:

> " Information like this makes it relevant for
>   me to remind that past performance is no
>   indication of future results."

In other words: Lots of luck. Speaking of luck, many mathematicians and economists have concluded that the best explanation for the success of the tiny number of mutual funds each year is that every year some fund money managers just get lucky. In 1988 *The Wall Street Journal* began an experiment inspired by economics professor Burton Malkiel's classic book, *A Random Walk Down Wall Street*. In the book, Dr. Malkiel theorized that "a blindfolded monkey throwing darts at a newspaper's financial pages could select a portfolio that would do just as well as one carefully selected by experts." *Wall Street Journal* staff members typically play the role of the monkeys (the *Journal* listed liability insurance as one reason for not going all the way and actually using live monkeys).

So who won the most contests and by how much? The pros won 61 of the 100 contests versus the darts. The pros losing 39% of the time to a bunch of darts certainly could be viewed as somewhat of an embarrassment for the pros. The pros barely edged the DJIA by a margin of 51 to 49 contests. In other words, simply investing passively in the Dow, an investor would have beaten the picks of the pros in roughly half the contests (that is, *without even considering transactions costs or taxes*).

The bottom line is that there was precious little difference between the performance of the pros and that of the monkeys, which lends a great deal of credence to Burton Malkiel's original thought experiment, the lesson of which, as far as we are concerned here, is that the class of mutual fund money managers fails to add any value for the class of individual investors. Why not?

Burton Malkeil used monkeys in his classic example to make his wider point that the money managers who do manage to outperform the market are lucky, just like a lucky monkey's darts will select stocks that outperform the market. Why can't we do better investing in actively managed mutual funds? Why can't the gains for the investor justify the costs? There are three main reasons why mutual fund managers fail to add value for shareholders:

- Their performance is based on their ability to pick stocks
- The fees are too high
- The structure of mutual funds constrains their growth

THE STOCK PICKER'S MERRY-GO-ROUND

One fundamental assumption behind actively traded mutual funds is that you're not managing the money in the fund unless you're trading in and out of stocks and trying to predict the future and time the market. The belief is that the money manager's job is to beat the market, and that the way to do this is to take advantage of his expertise in stock selection and market timing.

The constant pressure for mutual fund money managers to trade turns them into hyperactive traders in an effort to win short-term bets that end up delivering performance that out-paces the stock market as a whole. With the latest information technology and research teams at their disposal, they can also trade from industry to industry and sector to sector simultaneously. Some mutual funds have a high turnover rate. This means that they could sell their entire portfolio a little more than once a year, and for what? Active money management not only fails to deliver returns that outpace the market, but the end result actually lags *behind* the market. This super-accelerated trading is also the root cause of a fund's change of investment strategy. The fund manager can change direction at any time without seeking your approval. The fund money manager has to act as though he knows all the trends, so he can invest before others find out what he already knows, and then watch his stock picks shoot to the sky as the world unfolds just like he said it would. But he never gets it right, and he never seems to learn.

When the money manager faces the prospect of having to show that all of that trading only lost investors' money, in my experience some of them inevitably do each year, some of them will try to cover their poor performance with still more trading, to manipulate their returns for a couple of days, so things don't look as bad as they really are.

When all else fails, bring in smoke and mirrors

Not all managers manipulate their holdings to deceive their shareholders, but many do, so many in fact, that the tricks have come be known as "window dressing" and "portfolio pumping." The first practice adds high performing stocks right before the date the mutual fund must report its holdings in hopes of convincing investors that it had participated in the big run up of those stocks. The second technique is to pour major dollars into the stock directly before the reporting date in order to artificially increase the stock price. The price goes up, which shows a good return on the date of the reporting but then will immediately drop (and usually much farther) when the manager sells it off.

As you might expect, trading is not a free activity, and mutual funds pass on all the costs of every transaction to the individual investor. In a recent study entitled *The Role of Trading Costs*, it was found that trading costs pulled more capital from portfolios than commissions or expense ratios. The study found that the bigger the mutual fund, the higher the trading costs. "Trading costs," say the authors, "have an increasingly detrimental impact on performance as the fund's relative trade size increases."[20] You can't control market performance, but you can control how much you pay for your investments.

HIGH FEES KILL YOUR RETURNS

The sponsor of an actively traded mutual fund doesn't much care about the impact of hyperactive trading if only because he doesn't care that the shareholder—the individual investor—loses money. He only cares about the bottom line for the fund company. He wants the mutual fund to grow in assets so he can collect more fees.

One way to look at the history of actively traded mutual funds is as a tug-a-war between the mutual fund industry's effort to profit from extracting fees and the individual investor's need to have costs stay low enough to make the investment sensible.

Insensitivity to costs, coupled with the drive to extract fees adds up to a losing proposition for mutual fund investors. Fund fees reduce returns. Hidden costs include bid/ask spreads, direct trading costs that only show up in the net cost of a stock position after the cost of the trade has settled.

Visible costs include:

- Local adviser commissions, both loads and wrap fees—1.01%
- Expense ratios, including management fees, administrative fees, legal fees, custody costs—1.35%
- 12-b1 fees—.37%
- Wall Street brokerage fees (inside the fund)—1.32%
- Capital gains tax from excessive trading—amount will vary

The total pre-tax cost to the investor in the average active mutual fund comes to 4.5%. The figure does not try to include money lost to capital gains taxes. Outside of a tax sheltered retirement plan like a 401(k), the costs of taxes can be the most important expense to overcome. Regardless, the data shows that mutual funds started charging high fees and justifying those fees by talking about how great their money managers were at stock selection in the late 1970s and that overall fees and costs have gone up since then.

In 2009, for the first time since the mutual fund was introduced in 1932, the U.S. Supreme Court heard arguments in favor of giving investors the ability to successfully sue their funds for charging too much. The filing came from a group of law professors, industry legend John Bogle, the AARP, The Consumer Federation of America, and Solicitor General Elana Kagan, on behalf of the Securities and Exchange Commission.

DESIGN FLAWS MAKE WINNING VIRTUALLY IMPOSSIBLE

The mutual fund's mechanics are counterproductive. Conceivably, a money manager of an actively traded mutual fund could wake up one morning, and make a pledge to minimize trades and control costs. No matter how well intentioned the manager may be, he is stuck with the fund's structure. Since its arrival in 1932, the actively traded mutual fund has been in a constant state of repair. Over the years, it's been festooned with regulations and policies, imposed both voluntarily and at government's insistence. Currently, the mutual fund as handed down retains two fateful design flaws.

Ridiculous diversification constraints

By law, no stock position can represent more than 5% of an actively traded mutual fund. As well intentioned as the members of the committee who dreamed up this requirement may have been, the unintended consequence is devastating to the performance of a portfolio. Regulations say that the money manager cannot keep the stocks that start to do very well. The 5% rule chases out all the best stocks in the fund. Since the stocks that have appreciated most are the ones that must be sold, trading to meet diversification requirements lowers performance and triggers capital gains taxes also. This rule was actually made into a law —over 60 years ago.

Mindless redemption procedures

The second problem with the way mutual funds are made is the manner in which they give back money to shareholders, how they "honor redemption requests." Large amounts of investor dollars must always be diverted from the fund and set aside to provide money for shareholders who wish to quit the fund. That cash reserve must be large enough to handle normal outflows from the fund. The trouble starts when normal is not normal anymore—when there is a run on the fund, and large numbers of shareholders want out at the same time. On those occasions an awful snowball effect ensues. Since there is not enough cash on hand to accommodate the high demand for redemptions, money managers must sell off holdings—for whatever they can get—in order to come up with the cash for the shareholders who are cashing in their shares.

As if the mutual fund doesn't undergo enough trading at the hands of the stock picker, the structure of the fund forces trades that no one wants to make. The trading forced upon the fund at times when shareholders are leaving in large numbers only increases the magnitude and speed of the portfolio's collapse. No matter how they may be repackaged or re-branded, the fact remains that actively managed mutual funds are unable to overcome the most basic and fundamental obstacle: they cost too much.

The chances of your knowing the stated fees for the shares of mutual funds you purchase through your 401(k) are not good. According to a survey by the Transamerica Center for Retirement Studies, only 29% of employees said they knew how much they were paying in 401(k) fees. Forty-eight percent said they were unaware of the fees, and 23% were not sure what they were charged.[21]

That's why, for all their popularity, so called "target-date funds" may not live up to their promises. Target-date funds received a sharp spike in their press coverage amid the devastation of the market meltdown that signaled the great recession of 2008/09. It made news the way so many mutual fund products do: by performing so poorly that congressional hearings were called to find out what in the world went wrong.

TARGET-DATE FUNDS MISS THE POINT

Target-date funds have special features to make them appealing choices within a retirement plan. What is most special about a target date fund is that it automatically shifts its assets to become more conservative as the investor ages. One of the real problems with 401(k)-type plans is that they require participants to make many decisions and changes throughout the course of their participation in the plan. So policy makers and fund companies dug inside the plans and tried to automate as much of it as possible.

It was in this spirit of automation that fund companies came up with the idea of automatically shifting assets in a fund to ensure that as you age, you hold fewer risky "stocks" and more safe "bonds." The appeal is that once you select a fund, you can forget about it. Other than making contributions to build your balance, nearly all other investment decisions are made for you automatically. This gradual shift in the asset mix of a portfolio is known as the "glide path," because the increasing allocation to bonds as the target year approaches looks like a plane coming in for a landing. I have no quarrel with the idea of the glide path as such, as long as it does not shut down the discussion of what really matters when selecting funds for your retirement plans.

More important than any automated shifts in asset allocation is how the fund is being managed on a daily basis, and whether it is transparent and has low costs. If the participant in a 401(k) demands these things first, then a glide path portfolio could work well, assuming the "glide" accurately reflects the individual's situation. The trouble is that all the talk about shifting assets and target dates and glide paths can have the effect of changing the topic, leaving you with an actively managed mutual fund that has been around sometimes for a decade or more, performing poorly and charging high fees. Don't let the fancy wrapping around the same old products throw you off your game.

The huge problem with mutual funds is not alleviated by target funds, because success for the managers of those funds is the same as success for mutual fund executives generally. In either case, success is not about creating impressive investment returns; it's about amassing as huge a pile of assets as they possibly can. The bigger the pile of money, the more money they're going to make. That's the way fund companies generate greater profits. The way they define winning is at odds with the way you define it. Their goal can sometimes be to amass assets under management, not to develop a great investment record.

CHAPTER FIVE

THE DEATH OF THE AMERICAN PENSION: THE WEIGHT OF THE WORLD IS ON YOUR SHOULDERS, NOW WHAT?

They were supposed to be solutions for both employees and employers. Yet 401(k)-type plans have proven to be an insufficient weapon in the fight against the risks inherent in increased life expectancy, negative savings rates, Social Security's failure, and a market that crashes. It is not so much that the 401(k) plan is broken. The problem is that it has not had a chance to evolve into a viable alternative to traditional pensions. After all, when the 401(k) concept was first developed, no one had any idea that it would one day be presented as a viable option to traditional pensions. Yet studies show that the final vanquishing of traditional pensions by 401(k)-type plans is now inevitable.

401(k)-type plans will soon replace virtually all traditional pensions. Here is another perfect example of how the new generation needs to redefine retirement—pensions are gone. The new retirement plans must be placed at the center of the redefinition of retirement. In order to make the most of a 401(k) plan, a participant has to find out about how they work. How many Americans with a traditional pension could explain how they worked—their mechanics and the math behind them? Knowing how they worked had no relevance for making the most of them. It was just done for you. That was then. Now, such ignorance can jeopardize your quality of life in retirement.

The percentage of private sector employees covered by a defined-benefit plan (a traditional pension) fell from 61% in 1979 to 9% by the mid 2000s. The upshot of this nationwide shift is that the main risk of retirement savings—that misfortune could mean the money you contributed may not be there when it's needed—gets taken off the shoulders of the corporate sponsors and placed squarely on the shoulders of the individual.

> *For too many Americans, 401(k) plans have become little more than a high-stakes crap shoot. We are realizing that Wall Street's guarantees of predictable benefits and peace of mind throughout retirement was nothing more than a hollow promise."*
>
> –House Education and Labor
> Committee Chairman, George Miller

In this chapter we consider aspects of 401(k)–type plans

from the perspective of the individual participant. What is at stake in having a retirement plan that is an investment portfolio? What are the advantages and disadvantages? How can you tell a good 401(k)-type plan from a bad one? What are the important weaknesses in the new plans? How can you avoid common mistakes? What should you know about conflicts of interest between you and your investment product provider? What steps can you take to avoid corrupt practices that go on behind the scenes of some 401(k) plans?

The number of companies offering traditional pensions or "defined benefit" plans was shrinking even before the recession of 2008/09, but the downturn accelerated the transition. As Karen Friedman, policy director for the Pension Rights Center, commented in her Congressional testimony, "The market collapse has just proven how fundamentally flawed 401(k) plans are as a vehicle to provide retirement income." [22]

Originally, the idea of a 401(k) was not connected to retirement planning at all. It was devised rather as a means for executives to avoid paying taxes on their bonuses. 401(k)-type plans did not become available to all employees until 1980, when an entrepreneur developed a business model based on selling the idea to employers. [23]

Yet when non-executives began investing via 401(k)s, they were using them only to supplement their traditional pension plans. Indeed, it's hard to imagine the new idea ever getting off the ground had it been coupled with the elimination of company-sponsored pensions.

Yet no sooner did the 401(k) spread as an employee benefit than it began to take the place of pensions, something it was never intended to do. Alicia Munnel, Director of the Center for Retirement Research at Boston College, connects the plan's murky beginnings with its current failure:

> Even before the financial crisis, I was concerned about the ability of 401(k) plans to provide secure retirement income. They were not designed for that role. When 401(k) plans came on the scene in the early 1980s, they were viewed mainly as supplements to employer-funded pension and profit-sharing plans.
>
> We need a new tier of retirement income that would allow 401(k)s to return to their original role as a supplementary savings plan.[24]

Why have so may of us found the 401(k) story so compelling? Well, there are two stories in fact, one for the employees and one for the employers.

THE FIRST STORY: THE 401(K) PUTS YOU IN THE DRIVER'S SEAT

The 401(k) has a simple yet powerful story for employees.

It goes like this: Traditional pensions are from a bygone era, when you stayed with one company at one location for your entire career. Back then, your boss took out a little something from your paychecks and let it grow an average of 3% annually over 30 years. So much has changed since then! Why should you be forced to let your hard earned money sit in a company pension when you could take that same capital and invest it—tax free? Unlike the old-fashioned pension, the 401(k) is mobile. You take it with you wherever you go. What makes it mobile? Ownership. You own your 401(k). (As we will see in a few paragraphs, the ownership claim can be a stretch.)

Part of the reason we are attracted to the idea of the 401(k) plan is that it sounds like an advance in retirement planning that we want to be a part of. We value independence; the 401(k) offers it. We tend to distrust forces greater than ourselves when it comes to saving the money that we have earned. The 401(k) appears to confirm our sense that *we* know how best to manage the money we earn. The 401(k) seems to put us in the driver's seat. Finally, to boost the horsepower of your plan, your employer will do something unheard of in the traditional pension: they will match your contributions, usually dollar for dollar.

Of course, there's no mention in this story of any scientific or empirical data of any kind. The story has never really developed an empirical narrative at all. It grabs us at an emotional level. In fact, from the perspective of the individual investor, there is very little data anywhere to support the main talking points in favor of the 401(k) against traditional pension plans. Not that it matters to the story. After all, the 401(k) story does not make any propositions that data could disprove. It's not a story that gets better if you can prove what you say, if only because it does not make any verifiable claims to begin with. The appeal of the story comes from the sentiments it expresses, rather than any concrete arguments it puts forward. That's not to say that the efforts to shape comprehensive 401(k) plans have not used scientific methods to develop solutions.

Automatic participation and enrollment: Problem solved but not implemented

By the time 401(k)s began to proliferate nationwide in the early eighties, studies on success rates identified two huge problems. Many employees, far too many, never even bothered to enroll in their company's 401(k) plan. Among those who did take the time to enroll, only a small minority contributed as much as they needed to and, in fact, agreed to. The solution? Have the plan take care of both of these problems through simple automation. The idea is to provide a simple "flotation device" to keep the participation rates high.

There is definitely a consensus that automatic enrollment and automatic contributions should be a standard among the plan providers. Here is a case of a clear and simple application of basic scientific methods that diagnosed a problem accurately and then provided an effective remedy. Yet the pace of change here is remarkably slow. Charles Schwab's 401(k) division reported that thirty-two percent of the plans they administer now automatically enroll participants, up from 24% in 2007, and 10% have automatic savings increases, up from 6%.[25]

Retirement economist Teresa Ghilarducci, author of *When I'm Sixty Four: The Plot Against Pensions and How to Save Them*, says that these low participation rates are connected to employer costs, as the plans require more funding as more employees participate. She writes:

> **"** Despite knowing ways to increase enrollment, only 14% of employers providing 401(k) have adopted automatic enrollment—perhaps it works too well! What I mean to imply is that employers may not mind if employees opt out; firms save money when they do. Between 2002 and 2004, if all eligible employees had taken part in the employers' 401(k) plans, employers would have had to contribute 26% more to their plans than they did—that would have come to an annual total of $3.18 billion more contributions. Simple? Yes."[26]

You might say that the employer has an incentive not to push to hard for employee buy-in. On the other hand, it is important to remember the argument *against* automatic enrollment. That is, that automatic enrollment and automatic contributions amount to an involuntary exposure of employees' savings to risk. And it is the employees' new exposure to risk that brings us to the second 401(k) story, the one that the plan provider tells the employer.

THE SECOND STORY: THE 401(K) AS A WAY TO SHIFT THE RISK FROM YOU TO THEM

One finds no emotional appeals in the story that 401(k) plan providers tell to corporate sponsors. In place of ideas like independence, freedom, and ownership, the corporate 401(k) story focuses on transferring risk and reducing costs. The fundamental problem of pension plans, from the corporate perspective, is that we are all living longer, much longer, than we were when the pension plan developed its policies and assumptions. How can a company now guarantee income for workers in retirement for 30 years when they worked at the company for 20 years? 401(k)-type plans shift the risk from the company's balance sheets to the employees' retirement accounts.

Polling numbers show that many of us hold two opinions that contradict one another. Participants in 401(k) plans think the idea is great, but the actual outcomes have increased their worries that they will not have enough income to sustain them through retirement. The approval ratings for

401(k) plans continue to shoot through the roof, even while 71% of participants surveyed said they were very concerned about having enough income to meet their standard of living throughout retirement.

A NEW GENERATION OF RISK

Longevity risk for a new generation

Often defined as "the risk of outliving one's assets," longevity risk includes equity market risk, interest rate risk, inflation risk, timing risk, and conflict of interest risk. These risks were assumed or neutralized (to varying degrees) in the savings and payout phases of traditional pensions. The increase in anxiety over outliving one's assets should come as no surprise as 401(k) plans offer little, if any, protection against these risks. In addition to neglecting the over-arching risk of longevity and the risks included in it, the shift to 401(k) plans adds risks not seen before. Let's take a look at them.

Rule changing risk

The weaknesses and flaws of 401(k) plans are worrisome enough when all the pieces are in place and the employer's matching contributions enable real growth of retirement savings. The problem is that the employer's match is far from etched in stone. Many who were close to retirement in 2008 saw their 401(k) plans lose close to half its value only to discover that their employer decided to stop matching their contributions. The economic crisis has taken a significant toll on matching contributions to retirement plans. The trend raises questions about the ability of the current generation of working Americans to adequately fund their retirements.

So much for the vaunted "ownership" of the defined contribution plans as over and against the defined benefit plans. Just because people call you the king does not make you the king. What good is owning your 401(k) if you don't have control over how it's funded? By the end of 2009, a full one-third of employers cut back on or eliminated their 401(k) matches. In other words, the deal's off. For now. When will the matches start up again? No one really knows.

Of course, no one considered that the matches could be stopped with the snap of a finger. The ability to change the rules in hard times was a kind of open secret that gave increased security to the employers at the expense of the plan participants. Inevitably, vanishing matches will translate into decreases in participant contributions, as individuals lose their motivation, once the incentive of doubling their money is taken away. According to Janice M. Nittoli, Rockefeller Foundation Vice President, millions of people will consequently face difficult retirements.

When you lose the free money from your company, you're essentially losing a big chunk of return on your savings. That is another reality that distinguishes retirement for a new generation. If this happens to you, it may be wise to take the money you would normally contribute and put it to work elsewhere, such as paying down credit card debt, padding an emergency fund, or re-evaluating your retirement investment options all together. In order for 401(k) plans to work, even just as a supplement to pensions, which his how they were initially designed, "contributions need to be both sufficient and consistent," says Nittoli. At the end of 2007, the average 401(k) plan had a meager $18,942 in it.[27] For the time being, if employers continue to cut back or eliminate 401(k) matches, "Such a new norm would only trade today's individual sorrows for tomorrow's societal calamity."

Corruption risk

Traditional pensions are corporate-sponsored benefits, in a category with vacations and office parties; 401(k)s are products. Taking advantage of perks in the former category is not a risky proposition, while participation in the latter brings all the attendant risks of being a consumer in a marketplace. In 2008 for instance, two women sued Principal Financial Group, alleging that the firm used deceptive practices to get them to rollover their 401(k) assets. The suit says that Principal, which also held 401(k) accounts, contacted thousands of people in a manner that led them to believe they were talking to an account manager. In reality, they were talking to a commission-hungry sales person. The only funds that people were permitted to rollover into had extraordinarily high fees, including undisclosed compensation, the suit alleges:

> DES MOINES, Iowa (AP)—Principal obtained names and addresses of employees nearing retirement from Principal-managed 401(k) accounts. Letters were sent to pre-retirees as young as 58 "misleading them to believe they were dealing with their account manager who was looking out for their interests," the lawsuits said.

> The letters did not disclose that the phone number participants were directed to call was to sales agents at Princor Financial Services Corp., a Principal subsidiary broker/dealer rather than the Principal pension administration department.

An isolated case of rogue salesmen engaging in unethical practices for their own enrichment? Perhaps. Evidence, however, suggests that this particular illegal act stems from a general culture of conflicts of interest that has grown up around the high demand for 401(k) plans.

Conflicts of interest risk

All too often, employees are ripped off by the very consultants who are supposed to be advising them. Almost every major corporate employer utilizes the services of these providers. Supposedly, they have a fiduciary responsibility to place the interests of the employees above their own. The advice they give should be totally objective and free of conflicts. In the best cases, investment professionals live up to their responsibilities; in the worst, kickbacks, price gouging and bad investment advice abound.

A study by the Securities and Exchange Commission, entitled *Staff Report Concerning Examinations of Select 401(k) Plan Consultants,*[28] documents the conflicts of interest in numerous examples of downright reprehensible games being played with Americans' retirement dreams. It turns out that many 401(k) plan advisors have consulting relationships with both employers and the mutual funds they recommend for inclusion in the plan. The SEC study found that some plan providers host conferences at resorts for their corporate clients. The corporate plan sponsors get their tab picked up by the plan providers. Who are the speakers at these conferences? The money managers who run the funds that get recommended for inclusion in your 401(k) plan. They get charged a fee. The fee covers the "free" attendance of the company reps. And the conflicts of interest don't stop there.

Here is another example of the corrupt practices behind the scenes of the 401(k) business: Some providers "sell" software programs to the money managers whose funds are recommended for inclusion in your plan. The fees for these programs can be as high as $70,000, even though the same programs can be bought on the open market for two or three thousand dollars. That's simple pay-to-play corruption.

These scams make you mad—or they should—but do they have a direct impact on your retirement savings? Probably not. What does affect your personal bottom line, however, in a big way, is that these same 401(k) plans include endless lists of high-cost actively managed mutual funds. The money managers who swim in these waters are not in charge of low-cost, passively managed index funds or ETFs.

High fee risk

Offering a broad assortment of mutual funds does not improve performance. In fact, research suggests that too many investment options overwhelm participants and may actually reduce participation levels. The fees charged by most actively managed mutual funds simply cannot be justified when one looks at their long-term performance. Many investors in these funds pay a premium to under-perform the market.

Seemingly small differences in fee levels could add up to hundreds of thousands of dollars over time. The difference in expenses between an average equity income fund and a similar ETF could mean a substantial difference in the value of a portfolio over 30 years.

In 2007, Congress held hearings on the level of fees for 401(k) plans in the wake of a report that concluded employees often cannot understand or even find out what the fee is for having a 401(k). One percentage point can translate to a

serious erosion of your retirement money. A person investing $10,000 a year over 30 years and earning 6% per year,
for instance, would have more than $790,000 for retirement;
if those same $10,000 yearly contributions only earned 5%,
the sum would be $664,000.

SUMMING UP: GETTING THE MOST FROM YOUR 401(K)

Anyone who participates in a 401(k) plan faces the possibility of dealing with a sub-par service provider. But how do you
know? The most common visible weaknesses in 401(k) are:

- Poor communication—employees are left in the dark
- Lack of knowledge—managers do not know how to
  judge between plans
- Lack of responsibility—providers are not willing to
  acknowledge their fiduciary obligation on paper
- Lack of objectivity—commission and revenue shar-
  ing create conflicts of interest
- Lack of transparency—not clear on fees and costs
- Lack of investment options—offer only high-cost ac-
  tively managed mutual funds

The 401(k) plan is here to stay, and the best use for the
above review of its risks is to turn it upside down and formu-
late the essential elements of a good plan—one that helps
individuals cope with these risks in the most realistic way.
So, I believe the essential elements of an investor-centered
plan will:

- Be provided by a certified co-fiduciary
- Offer broadly diversified model portfolios that not only comply with all government regulations but also include low-cost index funds and exchange traded funds (ETFs)
- Provide automatic enrollment and contribution increases, and full online access to individual accounts
- Offer comprehensive education, including one-on-one consultations with an investment professional

There are still plenty of 401(k) plans across the country that offer only high-cost actively managed mutual funds. Is your plan among them? If so, do you know what the fees are for those mutual funds? If you do not, it will be impossible to evaluate the performance of your investments.

Even the best 401(k) you can imagine can only provide *supplemental income*. The outcome of investing in stocks is an unknown. Today, it would be risky to base your retirement plans on an investment whose outcome is fundamentally unknown. The value of every 401(k) plan in existence is always at the mercy of market crashes and economic cycles. That would be very troubling were the 401(k) expected to stand on its own. Happily, there are other planks to turn to in order to build up support for your 401(k). Perhaps you will want to ask yourself if you are willing to give up leaving a greater inheritance if you could have a greater amount of lifetime income. Or maybe another savings device would best mitigate longevity risk within the context of your personal retirement plan.

PART TWO

SHELTER FROM THE STORM:
THE REALITY OF RISK & THE
FIGHT FOR RETIREMENT

CHAPTER SIX

RETHINKING INVESTING AND RETIREMENT: THE TROUBLE WITH THE PHILOSOPHY OF BUY AND HOLD

If you want to retire with independence, it is absolutely critical to identify and understand as clearly as possible the various obstacles that you face. As we have seen in previous chapters, considering the impact of declining birth rates, a pension system in chaos, the sheer size of the retiring boomer generation, and our increasing life expectancy make it clear that no one who desires an independent retirement can afford to leave it to chance. You must take steps to turn the chaos into cosmos. The proliferation of risk in the current environment only increases the urgency of developing a plan and a discipline.

Yet, rejecting chance and deciding to build a plan introduces you to a whole new range of hazards. You decide to open an investment portfolio. Well, how do you create one, and what do you do with it once it's opened? This is the point at which most individuals turn to a professional investment adviser, a turn that leads them not only to a marketplace of products but of ideas also. As in any marketplace, the terrible ideas are mixed in with the ones that may have been right once but no longer apply, as well as the ones that are right for you. How do you discern the difference?

THE USES AND ABUSES OF BUY AND HOLD

Is buy and hold a dangerous idea or a dangerous *oversimplification of an idea*? It definitely has enjoyed widespread popularity. The idea is that once your portfolio has been designed, the thing to do is to hold those positions forever, no matter what the economic conditions (except for a yearly rebalancing act to return the portfolio to its initial mix of stocks and bonds). This idea is commonly known as *buy and hold*. The philosophy of buy and hold developed within the tradition of serious long-term investing. At the same time, it is important to be aware of a vulgarized version of the slogan.

BAD FAITH BUY AND HOLD

If you are advised to buy and hold actively managed mutual funds, all you are really holding are your shares in a particular investment/marketing company, since transactions within the portfolio are taking place at a furious pace. Though you may be under the illusion that you are a long-term buy and hold investor, the truth is that you are exposing your investment earnings to the risks and costs of the short-term speculations of a money manager under pressure to make trades.

How can you invest for the long term with a mutual fund whose money manager is a short-term investor? You cannot. In this context the admonition to buy and hold is little more than a device to ensure that an active mutual fund maintains the assets it has gathered no matter how poorly the fund manager performs. The wisdom of the buy and hold mantra has been hijacked and vulgarized to mean, in effect, "invest all you can in our funds, do not redeem your shares no matter what, do not ask questions."

SERIOUS BUY AND HOLD

By contrast, serious buy-and-holders want to protect their clients from the loser's game of over-trading. They do so by preaching the buy-and-hold alternative. That is why most of them replaced commissions with flat fees and one-by-one stock picking with diversified portfolios. It is also why, more recently, the serious buy-and-holders rejected actively managed mutual funds, as they saw that the fund managers' principles were flawed and recognized that the outcome for the investor would never justify the expense.

Originally, the buy and hold approach was developed as a way to protect the individual investor from the temptation of mistaking investing for gambling, or high stakes speculating. Financial practitioners of integrity preached buy-and-hold as a way to steer individuals clear of so called experts who claimed they could either time the market or select the right securities and thus provide gains that beat the market.

It is perhaps easy to forget that before the rise of mass investing in the early seventies, many individuals who wanted to invest did so by following a hot tip on this or that stock from a broker whose duties stopped at the end of a phone call. The secret to the brokers' tips was based on one of two claims: either they claimed to know the timing was just right, or they claimed to know about a particular stock that others did not. Reams of data and analysis have been amassed over the past 25 years that show beyond all reasonable doubt that the experts who receive fees from individuals for timing the market or selecting stocks cannot deliver on their most basic claims.

The main problem: Since compensation for the market timers and stock pickers consists of commissions per transaction, as long as transactions keep occurring, they cannot lose. So they have little or no incentive to recognize the folly of their ways.

BUY AND HOLD: A TRADITION OF EXCELLENCE

It is important to see how this trend of thinking represents a step forward for the investing profession, and for investors too. It is equally important to realize that there is no reason to believe it was the last step, and many reasons to see it as one step on the way to a truly investor-centered approach to portfolio investing.

The general proposition, "buy and hold", is a sensible remark that signifies a wise, emotion-sensitive approach to investing. The general buy and hold proposition is the cornerstone of a tradition of financial analysis and investment philosophy that that leads from investing legend Warren Buffet[29], to John Bogle[30], founder to Vanguard, to a stable of Nobel Laureates including Burton Malkeil[31] of Princeton, and Charles Ellis of Harvard.[32]

The founder of financial analysis and popular investment philosophy himself, Benjamin Graham first expressed the approach in simple terms in his Classic (also compact), "*The Intelligent Investor.*"[33] In addition to starting the genre of investment writing, Graham's book also provided one of the clearest warnings to individual investors ever written. The warning is this: Follow your emotions, you lose; resist the emotionalism that market gyrations evoke, you win. Sounds easy. Notice, however, that Graham goes on to say that the fortitude required to stick with an investment strategy is much more rare than you might think. According to Benjamin Graham, the investor who can pull it off will have to be, "a different sort of person from the rest of us ... not subject to the alternations of exhilaration and deep gloom that have accompanied the gyrations of the stock market for generations past." The ideas at the heart of the buy and hold adage, expressed by Benjamin Graham in 1949, are:

- Fight the temptation to let the herd mentality dictate your emotions
- Anticipate mass hysterias of panic and enthusiasm
- Look for opportunity when the herd is panicking
- Hesitate when the herd is itching to invest

An immediate and obvious consequence of not being "subject to the alternations of exhilaration and deep gloom that have accompanied the gyrations of the stock market" is a marked reduction in trading, a reduction in buying and selling, an overall reduction in activity.

Reacting to the ups and downs of the market by buying and selling is a "loser's game" to use a term that provided Nobel Laureate Charles Ellis of Harvard with the title of his excellent book first published in 1987. Better to remain disciplined within a long-term investment strategy than to throw your money away on trading costs in some vague scheme to outsmart the market. This is the wisdom of buy and hold—that its implementation has helped individuals to reject market timing, chasing returns, and stock picking is an entirely good thing.

Of course, at no time did Benjamin Graham suggest that buying and holding was equivalent to setting your portfolio on autopilot indefinitely. This notion has been oversimplified over time, and exploited by some in the investment community who would rather have clients who were willing to stop asking questions and simply "set it and forget it." Warren Buffet was named above as an advocate of buy and hold. That's true. But he would never accept the notion that the buy and hold approach can be reduced to a dogma that ties investors' hands *no matter what*.

Advocates of straight buy-and-hold would say that figure 6 below is a picture worth a thousand words.

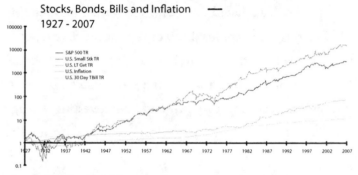

Stocks, Bonds, Bills and Inflation

Source: Ibbotson Associates

Figure 6

This way of measuring market risk focuses on your holding period. The idea here is that the longer you hold a portfolio of diversified stocks, the less likely your chance of losing money over the entire term. The problem is that, assuming you started investing at the age of 21, you would have been 104 years old in 2010. Incidentally, 1982 marked the beginning of one of the world's greatest bull markets; the year is commonly believed to be the start of the buy and hold era.

The picture worth a thousand words blurs over very important details: the elements of the picture that portray the real story. This story can be an awful tale about what happens to an individual whose retirement gets caught up in a severe downward blip, one of the many losing spikes that you barely notice in the 80-year chart.

WHAT'S WRONG WITH BUY AND HOLD?
THE REAL AND PRESENT DANGER OF BEING WIPED OUT

Perhaps you have heard someone say something like this: "All investing is a snap! Just buy some good stocks or mutual funds, sit back, and let it ride." In fact, the more you study the history of the stock market, the more you begin to understand the real dangers of buy and hold investing. A single bear market can destroy a large portion of your accumulated assets.

Booms and busts in the market cycle

Nobel Laureate Paul A. Samuelson once observed: "The longer you own stocks, the greater the risk of a devastating loss." His insight would seem to have fallen on deaf ears. Today, mutual fund companies, the financial press, and many professional investment advisors appear to have convinced the majority of investors to accept the "let it ride" philosophy.

On average, bear markets come along every four or five years. Why would anyone just assume that they could withstand all the market crashes that stand between them and their retirement? Any single downturn can result in losses of 20%. How many times can an investor afford such a loss? Three times? Four times? Five? ... Here we see the truth in Professor Samuelson's remark. The longer you hold, the more likely it is that such a fall will occur. Your stock market investment grows riskier, not safer, with time. Another way of putting it is to say that when it comes to investing in stocks, time is not your friend.

The bear markets of 2008/09 slashed portfolio values an average of 47%. However, there were declines of 86%, 54% and 48% during the past century. In order to find these bleak realities, you have to zero in on the market's time line. Figure 7 shows that if we had bought and held the Dow Jones Industrial Average from the 2000 to 2008, we would be down 19.78%.

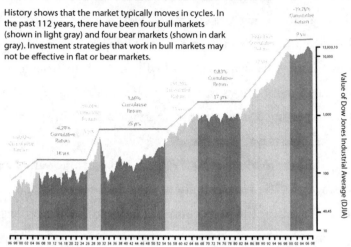

Dow Jones Historical Trends

History shows that the market typically moves in cycles. In the past 112 years, there have been four bull markets (shown in light gray) and four bear markets (shown in dark gray). Investment strategies that work in bull markets may not be effective in flat or bear markets.

Source: Graph created by Rydex/SGI using data from www.dowjones.com

Figure 7

Had you invested $100,000 in the stock market in January of 1973, your investment would have shrunk to $51,800 in just 21 months—a loss of 48.2%. Assuming you were able to continue your buy and hold strategy, you would have waited another seven and a half years just to break even.

You can easily see the risk that lurks in the stock market once you mark off the bull and bear cycles for the same time period. A bull market is defined as an upward-trending market and occurs when each successive high point is higher than the previous one. A bear market, or downward-trending market, occurs when a trend does not rise above the previous high.

No doubt, it is important to look at the longer history of the markets. Nevertheless, a closer look at shorter time intervals, as we have illustrated here, reveals that the Dow moves in cycles. Over the last 112 years, the average cycle lasted about 13 years, and coming off a 17-year-strong bull market that ended in 2000. Figure 8 below looks at the S&P 500 during the period December 31, 1996 through December 31, 2008.

S&P 500 Index at Inflection Points

Source: Standard & Poors, First Call, Compustat, FactSet, JP Morgan Asset Management

Figure 8

The years included in the preceding chart have yielded generally flat returns with a spike late in 2006 and continuing to fall since 2007. It is impossible to predict precisely when these cycles will occur; still, it is crucial to be aware of the current market cycle that you are in at any given time. The example speaks for itself, to be sure. Yet it also makes a much larger point.

There have been many other periods of decline throughout history, and there will no doubt be more periods of market decline in the future. Is a 100-year horizon relevant? How likely is it that a painful market decline will coincide with your retirement timing? As the famous economist Maynard Keynes wrote regarding the gap between historical statistics and investors who live in the real world: "In the long run, we're all dead."

In other words, *context determines risk*. For example, risk for a global financial analyst is different from risk for an individual whose goal is a secure retirement. The global analyst sees the downward cycles as insignificant dips in an upward pattern; the individual as so many catastrophes, should he—or she—fail to react. Both are right: the meaning of risk in the one arena is different from the meaning of risk in the other.

BRINGING RISK BACK TO THE REAL WORLD

The meaning of risk depends on the context in which it is used. What "risky" means in one context is different from what it means in the other. For individuals who invest long-term with retirement in mind, risk means what they can stand to lose. And this is exactly where the strict buy and hold idea falls down, where it becomes extreme and fundamentalist.

To be a pure buy and holder, you are not allowed to use the word "risk" as it applies to your particular life goals and material reality. Risk, they will insist, is being out of the market, and not being in when things turn around. That may be a statistically verifiable proposition, if placed in a wide enough time frame. But it's not the meaning of risk that is most relevant to the individual who wants to grow old with peace of mind.

In the end, it's just plain bullheaded. You can always take a picture of the market with the widest possible lens and see a positive trend that projects a sense that there is nothing to worry about once you invest. Of course, it is a sensible and empirically verifiable proposition that the market trends up over the long term. Why invest in it for the long term otherwise? The question is, *what relevance does the big picture of market increase have for individuals?*

One of Warren Buffet's most famous sayings is: "Be fearful when others are greedy, and greedy when others are fearful." You can't follow that advice by setting your portfolio on autopilot.

Successful investing in the stock market takes more than a single decision to buy certain mutual funds or a basket of stocks. It requires many important adjustments as market conditions change. Optimistic predictions from the so-called experts of Wall Street make interesting commentary, but do little to protect your assets when the stock market falls. No one knows the future; nevertheless, what is knowable is that the "let it ride" dogma will not preserve your assets in the next serious market decline. Before moving on to discuss portfolio investing 2.0 solutions, let's pause for a second to consider an objection to our discussion so far.

THE BUY AND HOLDER'S OBJECTION
AND MARKET TIMING

"You are contradicting yourself. You reject market timing as a loser's game, yet you advocate reacting to dire economic factors. That's just another kind of market timing. You should take your own medicine and realize that no one can successfully time the market. You end up succumbing to the very temptation you warned against."

The objection above suffers from the same extremism as the dogma it seeks to defend—that is, the fundamentalist claim that buy and hold can never waiver, or it's no longer buy and hold. Market timing is a *specific practice* with specific claims and, most importantly, specific fees and other costs. The individual investor engages in market timing either on a do-it-yourself platform or with the advice of a "professional." In either case the same result awaits.

The money it costs to time the market may cancel out the money gained by timing it. Sometimes, there is no money gained by timing the market over any significant period of time anyway, so the loss for the individual is actually two-fold.

In the objection above, market timing means something far less clear. There, the meaning of market timing gets stretched, to include *any reaction at all.* No reacting. Ever. No matter what. No exceptions. None.

If you followed through on the logic of this extreme

view, it would not be wise to *ever* open an investment portfolio in the first place! After all, such an act will have to include *some* consideration of the day it should be opened. And that would constitute an attempt to time the market. The point is, if everything is market timing, then nothing is. In the end, the objection doesn't make sense.

Setting your portfolio on autopilot is not a sure sign of prudence anymore than sitting back and watching your retirement savings evaporate a year before you retire is a virtue. To be a true follower of orthodox buy and hold, you have to ignore the risks of a catastrophe.

"RISK IS WHAT I DON'T KNOW."

What did Warren Buffet mean when he wrote, "Be fearful when others are greedy, and greedy when others are fearful." Well, it is not an exhortation to go to bed filled with the emotion of fear or greed during certain economic cycles. Fear and greed are to be reflected in changes in your investment portfolio. Mr. Buffet chooses the words *fearful* and *greedy* to denote actions: be fearful—decrease your exposure to equities; be greedy—recalibrate your assets and beef up on stocks.

Is Buffet's quote an argument for market timing? Of course not. There is no mention of the market at all in fact—only investors' reactions to it. To be sure, Warren Buffet has also written the following: "I like to hold a company forever, and I think most American' should too." There is no contradiction here. The message is this: approach investing as a buy and hold proposition, but by all means, take advantage of bargains, and whatever you do, avoid catastrophe. Warren Buffet also provided one of the best definitions of risk from the perspective of an individual investor: "Risk is what I don't know."

In general, a buy and hold approach is a rational reaction to media provocateurs who stoke greed and fear, or brokers who try to churn portfolios to generate commissions. The danger of catastrophic loss comes when buy and hold is stripped of all nuance—when misinformed pundits and professionals try to twist a sensible attitude into an absolute article of faith, and make you feel weak or uninformed simply because it occurs to you that your money may not be able to survive severe market downturns.

Recent research at the University of Chicago shows that individual investors do not lag in performance because they are too emotional. The poor returns they earn come precisely because they are on autopilot.[34] The next chapter starts by getting to the bottom of the whole buy and hold debate by going back to where it all began, within the development of financial theory, and to the first full conception of portfolio design. In short, Chapter Seven reviews the financial theory behind the discussion of the uses and abuses of buy and hold in order to create a safer and more prosperous definition of retirement.

LONG-TERM INVESTING AND RETIREMENT 2.0: SOLUTIONS FOR A NEW GENERATION

A decade after Benjamin Graham presented the philosophy of investing to a popular audience, Harry Markowitz published a book that everyone who says a word about portfolios for individual investors either argues with or against, whether he knows it or not. In 1959, Harry Markowitz published *Portfolio Selection*,[35] in which he asserted that investors expect to be compensated for taking risk. His groundbreaking work in portfolio construction won Markowitz his share of a Nobel Prize in Economics in 1990. His book was nothing less than an attempt to bring scientific method to the art of portfolio design. His attempt succeeded and he became the founder of modern portfolio theory (MPT).

BACK TO THE ROOTS OF THE MODERN PORTFOLIO

It would be difficult to overstate the influence of MPT's core principles on the manner in which investments are managed today. Markowitz's application of social science to portfolio design brought clarity and simplicity to concepts that are now cornerstones in long-term investing, including the connection between risk and return, diversification, asset allocation, and asset correlation. Markowitz's statistical discoveries yielded firm investing principles, none of which have ever been disproved. The following is a list of the six most important principles:

MODERN PORTFOLIO THEORY'S 6 ESSENTIAL INSIGHTS

1.) Investors are risk averse. The only acceptable risk is that which is adequately compensated by potential portfolio returns.

2.) Markets are efficient. For the most part, markets are fairly priced. It is virtually impossible to know ahead of time (with any degree of certainty) the next direction of the market as a whole or of any individual security.

3.) The portfolio is always more important than individual security selection. The appropriate allocation among asset classes (stocks, bonds, cash etc.) will have far more influence on long-term portfolio results than the selection of individual securities.

4.) Investing should be for the long term. Investment horizons of ten years or more are critical to investment success because it allows the long-term characteristics of the markets to surface.

5.) Every level of risk has an optimal allocation of asset classes that will maximize returns. Conversely, for every level of return there is an optimal allocation of asset classes that can be determined to minimize risk.

6.) Allocating investments among assets with low correlation to each other reduces risk if they're held long. Correlation is the statistical term for the extent to which two assets are similar to one another.

The six principles come together to express an overall effort to limit the risk of investing. Right away, the selection of individual stocks takes a backseat to the idea of allocating assets to control risk while maximizing gain. The next thing to go is market timing. It simply does not fit in the long-term equation of a diversified portfolio of assets allocated across a range of asset classes. The challenge for today's investor is to make sure the one designing the portfolio can deliver on the promises of diversification, while taking into account the unique nature of your individual financial goals.

It is not hard to see how the principles of investing for the long term in order to give the market patterns time to emerge, coupled with the primacy of asset allocation over individual securities selection, could trickle down to the public in the form of a simple slogan like "buy and hold." Yet neither those two principles, nor any of the others for that matter, expresses any kind of a mandate for such a black and white approach. MPT opened up vast trajectories of prosperity to individual investors when it showed the world how to measure diversification. The discovery meant that investment vehicles could be developed by professionals and then provided to the public. The investor class was born.

The method of measurement was called correlation, and it is the key pivot point for the move from the first generation of portfolio design to its current refinements.

MAKING LONG-TERM INVESTING POSSIBLE FOR EVERYONE: DIVERSIFICATION AND CORRELATION

MPT's most impressive contribution to portfolio design was its method of diversification and the power of correlation as a way to measure it. It is important to remember that both of these concepts come from the real world, and that MPT was simply trying to explain them using math and statistics. It's easy enough to find examples of these concepts at work in the everyday world. For example, street vendors rely on their ability to diversify. Vendors often sell unrelated products such as umbrellas and sunglasses. Initially, that may seem odd. Yet, by diversifying the product line in this way, the vendor reduces the risk of losing money on any given day. Rain or shine, the vendor prospers, because umbrellas and sunglasses have a very low correlation.

The bottom line of diversification is that assets with low correlation reduce risk of loss. Effective diversification depends on correlation—a statistical measure of how two assets move in relation to each other.

Assets with low correlations move in the same direction, up or down, but at different rates. If one asset falls a great deal, the other might fall just a little. Assets with negative correlations move opposite from one another. When one of them produces returns that are above average, the other's returns tend to fall below average. The best way to minimize your risk of investment loss is to own assets with low correlations. Negative correlations are even better.

New realities, however, have left received views of diversification in the dust. The traditional list of asset classes developed by Markowitz over 50 years ago, perhaps not surprisingly, no longer provides the low correlation it once did. Nevertheless, the original list of nine asset classes is still unquestioned by many professionals who design and manage portfolios. Meanwhile, computer technology has allowed for ever more precise measurements, not only of asset correlation but also of new asset classes.

A word about the title of this chapter will help clarify our purpose moving forward. This chapter uses the term "2.0" to underscore that rethinking portfolio design does not entail or even suggest a rejection of current best practices. "2.0" tells you that the platform is new yet not entirely so—as it builds upon what came before. Both the weaknesses of the first generation of portfolio design and the strengths of portfolio design 2.0 are all part of the natural evolution of portfolio theory. "2.0" refers to the second generation of portfolio construction that seeks to provide more robust asset allocation and to reinterpret risk and diversification for a wired world. Portfolio design 2.0 depends on the vocabulary developed by modern portfolio theory that has served investors extremely well over the past 50 years. Whenever you come words like, asset allocation, diversification, correlation, risk and return, you are witnessing the legacy of modern portfolio theory.

PORTFOLIOS IN THE POST-MODERN WORLD: RISK TAKES CENTER STAGE

Today's critics of MPT object to its abstract definition of risk. Fifty years ago, the authors of MPT understood quite well many of its limitations. Modern computer technology wasn't available to them, and the calculations necessary to perform the mathematic functions were exceedingly complex. What takes minutes today would have taken months to calculate then. Trying to quantify risk, for instance, with pre-computerized models strapped portfolio design with a very limited range of options. As a result, a generic model was utilized and remains more or less in place.

The idea that risk is the same for everyone has the same problems of older economic models that presupposed that all individuals will act in their best interest, since it is rational to do so. Both theories effectively level the individual, stripping away particular needs, goals, sentiments, and risk tolerance. Consequently, MPT does not bother to ask the individual what risk means to *him*. MPT assigns an abstract definition of risk to a hollow investor, whose objective is always the same: to maximize the expected return for a given level of risk. So for instance, a 40 year old who claims to have moderate risk tolerance in 2010 would be advised to take the same risks as a 40 year old with the same risk tolerance in 1970. MPT does not take into account that the 40-year old from 2010 can afford far less risk than the 40-year old from 1970, who, as we have seen, typically could count on two checks arriving each month, one from a solid pension plan and the other from a Social Security system that provided a good return on its contributions.

Critics of MPT want to rip the idea of risk out of abstract theories and ask a specific question that has no universal answer. The question is: what rate of return must be earned to accomplish specific goals with minimum risk. Risk then, is possibility that you will not achieve your goal. Risk is real again. The challenge for the critics of MPT is how to *refine* Markowitz' theory, how to develop a more flexible investment strategy that centers on what risk means to individual retirement plans, how to modernize that approach to include truly negatively correlated assets in the portfolio. These efforts have come to be known as post-modern portfolio theory (PMPT).

For instance, PMPT portfolios adjust their investment

mandates so that they will be better focused on macroeconomic conditions and be able to respond to adverse market conditions in the future and retain investor trust.

RETHINKING CORRELATION

The problem is that today, correlations change and converge with increasing frequency. As an example, consider large U.S. stocks versus emerging-market stocks. The traditional measures show them to have a low correlation. In fact, in 2008, emerging-market stocks were murdered. The MSCI Emerging Markets Index dropped 53% from January to November 2008, compared with 33% for the S&P 500. Traditional diversification within the original list of nine asset classes not only failed but also dragged you down more.

The same thing happened if you invested in smaller stocks to counterbalance larger stocks, or bought value stocks to counterbalance a growth portfolio. When stock prices fall, the correlations between these sets of assets rise. In other words, in down markets, all types of stock investments decrease in value all at once.

A BROADER ASSET ALLOCATION MENU

Expanding the number of asset classes, both positively and negatively correlated to the market, may allow more possibilities to lower your risk and increase reward potential. Figure 9 includes asset classes such as hedge funds, commodities, managed futures and real estate investment trusts.

Additional assets create more robust diversification. For example, if the S&P 500 Index were to experience a down year, one would expect an equity inverse strategy pegged to the index to potentially be up by a comparable compound-adjusted amount.

Achieve True Diversification

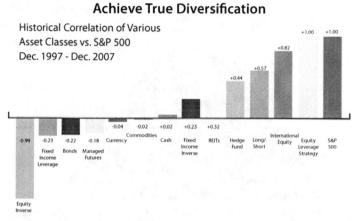

Historical Correlation of Various Asset Classes vs. S&P 500 Dec. 1997 - Dec. 2007

Source: Calculated by Rydex Investments using information from Bloomberg.com, Barclays.com and StandardAndPoors.com

Figure 9

How about commodities? Commodities historically perform counter-cyclically to stocks and bonds and, when added to a portfolio, can act as a hedge against inflation.

By complementing your portfolio of domestic equities, bonds, and international equities with some specialized investments, you may have the potential to better diversify and take advantage of changing market conditions. This innovation would reapply one of modern portfolio theory's most basic principles, that of asset allocation.

In 1991, a study determined that more than 90% of an investor's return was directly attributed to the way investments were diversified among various asset classes. The results of their landmark study, displayed in figure 10, confirm MPT's insight into the centrality of asset allocation.

Asset Allocation Drives Performance

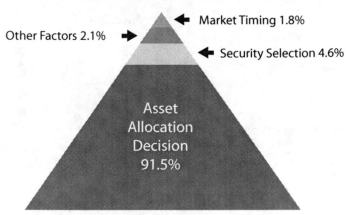

Source: Brinson, Singer and Beebower, 1991

Figure 10

The security selection decision—whether to invest in stock A or B—had little impact (only 4.6%) on the portfolio's return.

Unfortunately, many novice investors spend far too much time searching for the "hot" investment of the day rather than reviewing whether their investments support a solid asset allocation framework.

This is the part of modern portfolio theory that the serious buy-and-hold crowd got right. They are right to shun high levels of trading in an effort to either time the market or select the right stock.

What they fail to recognize is that risk must be understood as what it means to the individual investor. Those who are unlucky enough to be on the brink of retirement—or worse, those who were already retired—just as the market tanks will find themselves making radical adjustments to their retirement plans in order to get by.

The enlargement of the list of asset classes we have been discussing has already been analyzed and implemented by leading academics and successful asset managers, most notably for university endowments and foundations. Lately, the same changes that have met with success in these domains have been crossing over into portfolio design for individual investors. In what follows, we introduce these efforts and consider how they can contribute to an overall redefinition of retirement.

DAVID SWENSEN

David Swensen is responsible for managing and investing the University's endowment assets and investment funds, which total about $17 billion. He is chiefly notable for having invented what has become known as "The Yale Model" which is an application of Modern Portfolio Theory. The Yale Model as developed by David Swensen is described in his book *Pioneering Portfolio Management*. It consists of dividing a portfolio into five or six roughly equal parts and investing each in a different asset class. Central in the Yale Model is broad diversification and an equity orientation, avoiding asset classes with low expected returns such as fixed income and commodities.

Particularly revolutionary at the time was his recognition that liquidity is a *bad* thing to be avoided rather than a good thing to be sought out, since it comes at a heavy price in the shape of lower returns. The Yale Model is thus characterized by relatively heavy exposure to asset classes with lower liquidity compared to more traditional portfolios.

Seven years after his book on institutional investing, Swensen wrote a book to clarify the limits of applying his approach to endowments to individual investing.

Swensen recommends that you do not attempt to cobble together a portfolio that mirrors the Yale endowment. Rather, the individual investor has to guard against the temptation to jump into expensive actively traded mutual funds, to reject stock picking, and to focus on asset allocation, all core values of traditional modern portfolio theory. Swensen explains that he was disappointed to discover that the costs of actively managed mutual funds make it impossible for individual investors to pursue the strategies that he employs in his Yale endowment fund. He says that his active style is on one end of the spectrum and that individuals should invest on the other side of the spectrum. Since mutual funds are so expensive and since fund money managers trade without worrying about the tax impact on shareholders, the best way to build a portfolio is with passively managed, low cost index funds.

Swensen's advances, which you can call PMPT if you like, are steeped in the principles of MPT. In fact, Swensen reiterates some of MPT's founding principles with great style:

SWENSEN SPEAKS

On mutual funds

- "Overwhelmingly, mutual funds extract enormous sums from investors in exchange for providing a shocking disservice."
- "Overwhelming evidence proves the failure of the for-profit mutual-fund industry."
- "The entire mutual fund industry has failed. The clients lost, and the people who run the mutual funds made a lot of money. That's scandalous. It's a failure of the system."

On asset allocation

- "Asset allocation is the tool that you use to determine the risk and return characteristics of your portfolio. It's overwhelmingly important in terms of the results you achieve. In fact, studies show that asset allocation is responsible for more than 100 percent of the positive returns generated by investors."

On stock picking

- "There's no way that spending a few hours a week looking at individual securities is going to equip an investor to compete with the incredibly talented, highly qualified, extremely educated individuals who spend their entire professional careers trying to pick stocks. It's just not a fair fight. You know who's going to win before the bell rings."

Foundations and endowments can teach advisors strategies for constructing and maintaining retirement income portfolios. After all, the investor's vision coincides with the ultimate goal of an endowment manager—less risk and higher return. Every endowment manager has two goals. "If you are going to be a good steward of endowment assets," Swensen explains, "you need to care both about preserving the purchasing power of the portfolio and about providing as much for the operating budget as you possibly can."

RETIREMENT AS YOUR PERSONAL ENDOWMENT

The first thing to realize is the similarity of the tasks faced by asset managers of a foundation or endowment, and individuals who seek an independent retirement. By law, every foundation has to give away at least 5% of their assets each year. The challenge is to grow principal to keep pace with inflation, so they can meet commitments to grantees and cover operating expenses. That will be your challenge in retirement as well, where the general rule of thumb is that you will extract 4% of your assets each year.

Laurence Siegel, director of research in the investment division of the Ford Foundation, put it this way: "The problems of the retired investor and of the endowed institution are very closely related. Both seek to produce an income stream that grows with inflation." Of course, we must be cautious in what we take away from this parallel.

In fact, most investors can't act like the Ford Foundation or like the Harvard or Yale endowments—they just don't have enough money to deal with the assets that cannot be traded in and out of like stocks can. Swensen said it best: "Because of the enormous difficulty in identifying and engaging superior active managers, prudent investors avoid asset classes that derive returns primarily from market-beating strategies."[37]

3 PRACTICAL APPLICATIONS OF ENDOWMENT WISDOM FOR RETIREMENT INVESTING

- Wealth preservation is more important than growth: Be aware of your risk tolerance.
- Provide necessary capital to maintain your lifestyle.
- Determine how much you can spend from year to year.
- Do not box yourself into a narrow set of asset classes simply because conventional wisdom says to do so.

3 PRINCIPLES THAT APPLY TO BOTH
ENDOWMENTS AND RETIREMENT

- Seek true diversification.
- Avoid volatile asset classes.
- Rebalance aggressively.
- Don't try to outsmart the market.

One insight that *can* be carried over from his Yale Model to thinking about retirement is his principle of asset management. The way he managed assets was to be less dependent solely on domestic stocks and mutual funds and more diversified to alternative investments. This is really for risk management as stock, bond, and international asset allocations have become more correlated over the last 20 years.

What individuals concerned about retirement can learn from Swensen's Yale Model is not what to invest and where, not the specific asset allocation, but rather the general strategy for avoiding costs and achieving real correlation. It is in this way that Swensen represents a refinement of Modern Portfolio Theory. More broadly, we can take Swensen's adventures into new asset classes as inspiration to create new income streams for ourselves in retirement.

The only reason many of these different assets are called "alternative" is simply because there was no way to allocate them in portfolios before the advent of computers. Just as Swensen re-examined allocation strategy and changed what had become irrelevant or what had been passed by with computers, so the redefinition of retirement requires that we re-examine the traditional income sources and see if we can't do better.

Ivy League Examples

Harvard		Yale	
12%	Domestic Equity	12%	Domestic Equity
19%	Foreign equity: Emerging equity Developed equity	15%	Foreign equity: Emerging equity Developed equity
13%	Fixed income	4%	Fixed income
31%	Real assets: Commodities inflation-indexed bonds Real estate	27%	Real assets: Commodities inflation-indexed bonds Real estate
13%	Private equity	17%	Private equity
17%	Absolute return	25%	Absolute return

Source: *Smart Money*, September 2007

Figure 11

With mutual funds' cumbersome regulations, efficient rebalancing is not even possible. So if trading occurs at all regularly, it's only because the manager is engaging in securities selection or market timing. Not so with a portfolio designed with alternative assets. The dynamic re-allocation or aggressive rebalancing is possible because of a new clarity regarding correlation, tools for measuring it that have advanced exponentially.

REDEFINING RETIREMENT: REVIEW AND RESOURCES

If the last market bust of 2008/09 had been less of a melt-down and more of a moderate correction, the same challenges would all still be waiting. The most worrisome among these are the most entrenched and irrevocable. The aging boomer generation, our new longevity, and the closing of the traditional pension plan mean the new retirement requires income replacement in order to counter-act unstoppable trends that spell trouble for funding retirement. For a time, many boomers saw their skyrocketing home values as replacement income for retirement. Also for a time, many boomers saw the positive impact of a bull market on their 401(k) and thought they had found another way to replace retirement income. In fact, boomers saw their investment returns and their real estate appreciation as savings—so much so that they suspended the actual act of saving. No generation on record has ever saved less.

I have used several examples from the great recession of 2008 to shine a light on aspects of trends, behaviors, retirement plans, investment philosophies and portfolio designs that have been tearing the fabric of retirement for some time. Of course, the great recession is not the problem; it is simply an exceptionally serious market crash. The larger point is that since we have every reason to believe that market busts will become more frequent, retirement planning should focus on real risks, and keep an eye out for over-simple formulae and unrealistically optimistic assumptions about market returns. The risks, both apparent and hidden, of not meeting your retirement goals have been there for some time.

That's why I thought it was important to introduce the basics of modern portfolio theory (MPT) and recent innovations that fall under the category of post-modern portfolio theory (PMPT). Granted, these are advanced topics, and I have only just begun to scratch the surface of the subject matter. It is my hope that you will continue reading on the topic, as MPT and PMPT are sure to continue to emerge in mainstream talk about investment decision-making. PMPT is a risk-centered way of allocating assets, and as such it is not something that people want to discuss while the market is booming. The work that PMPT advocates have done to develop a richer understanding of risk has been going on for roughly a decade. They did not receive much of a hearing though, not until the financial crisis hit in 2008, and suddenly everyone wanted to know why their portfolios were not better protected.

In some cases, the new sensitivity to risk has led to portfolio models that rebalance monthly to stay on top of diversification and keep correlations low, and to clean out overvalued assets and pick up others that are undervalued. Often, these new models are based on highly advanced computer algorithms that churn out the monthly rebalancing strategies. Aware of the huge problems of mutual funds, these new models create baskets of stocks using low cost index funds and exchange-traded funds, (ETFs).

Focusing on risk is not glamorous. It can get complicated. We would much rather believe that there is nothing to worry about. Hopefully, the silver lining in the great recession of 2008 will be that it lights a fire under the seats of individual investors who want to take steps to secure their retirement.

Actively traded mutual funds have made it through booms and busts and there is no reason to suppose that they will be abandoned. But the main point against them—that their outcomes for investors cannot justify the expense—could never be clearer to the layperson who has seen their fees go up just as performance was the worst its been in 60 years. The crash of 2008 was so severe, that for the first time, financial advisers who used them in their practices started reconsidering.

The post-2008 climate made it clear that the 401(k) could no longer be presented as the great culmination of the American pension plan. Yet, experts have been warning about the risks of the new retirement plans for years. Their warnings were largely ignored until they could be no longer. Everyone now sees that the new retirement plans' superiority over traditional pension plans is by no means self-evident. Nevertheless, for the foreseeable future, 401(k)-type plans will be a fundamental building block for the new retirement.

All the criticism and analysis of 401(k) plans has one end: to get the most out of them, and then to build up other income streams around them. This task of making everything in the retirement system work for you as best as possible, while you recognize the parts of the system that you can no longer count on is the building up of your retirement scaffolding. There has never been a better time to make the case for redefining retirement. The old three-legged retirement stool is no longer a metaphor with any traction.

Retirement redefined includes a new skepticism of conventional diversification claims. Globalization has made it much harder to mix assets that have a low correlation to each other. Today, the idea that a collection of stocks and bonds that includes 95% domestic equities is sufficiently diversified is just plain false. Real negative correlation can only be achieved by investing in what have been called alternative assets, which is a term already outdated. There is nothing alternative about them. Better to refer to this approach as *all asset allocation*, so to make clear that it is not merely a strategy that you may elect to try. Real diversification starts with baskets of stocks and bonds that include domestic stocks, real estate investment trusts, Treasury bonds, inflation protected securities, foreign developed-market stocks, and emerging-market stocks. And the low correlations are sustained by disciplined rebalancing based on strict decision-making criteria developed around your specific risk tolerance.

With the traditional retirement income streams all drying up, the need to replace them has never been more pressing. In this context, Social Security's new irrelevance pushes us to a specific redefinition of retirement.

Instead of relying on Social Security benefits, realize that they have already started to be cut, and more such trimming back is inevitable. So Social Security becomes less important than *self-security*. We have to set Social Security aside—as if it did not even exist—and ask: Can I afford to retire? Building up your retirement scaffolding without the help of Social Security puts a new accent on risk, and focuses on the minimum you would need to survive a retirement spanning 30 or 40 years.

For instance, you may decide that the best way to react to the eclipse of Social Security is to plan to convert your retirement plan's *lump sum* into a fixed annuity that guarantees a certain amount of monthly income for the rest of your life. Does your situation warrant adding an annuity module to your retirement scaffolding? That will depend on many variables that are specific to your goals and assets. But now—armed with a redefinition of retirement—you're prepared to ask the right questions!

RESOURCES FOR REDEFINING YOUR RETIREMENT

BOOKS

The following is a selected list of outstanding books from the world's best minds on their subjects.

A Random Walk Down Wall Street: The Time-Tested Strategy for Successful Investing (Revised and Updated) by Burton G. Malkiel (Paperback - Dec 17, 2007)

Against the Gods: The Remarkable Story of Risk by Peter L. Bernstein (Paperback - Aug 31, 1998)

Common Sense on Mutual Funds: New Imperatives for the Intelligent Investor by John C. Bogle (Paperback - Oct 19, 2000)

Essays of Warren Buffett by Lawrence A Cunningham (Paperback - April 9, 2002)—Import

Fooled by Randomness: The Hidden Role of Chance in Life and in the Markets by Nassim Nicholas Taleb (Hardcover - Oct 14, 2008)

The Black Swan: The Impact of the Highly Improbable by Nassim Nicholas Taleb (Hardcover - April 17, 2007)

The Intelligent Investor: The Classic Text on Value Investing by Benjamin Graham (Hardcover - May 3, 2005)

The Intelligent Investor: The Definitive Book on Value Investing. A Book of Practical Counsel (Revised Edition) by Benjamin Graham, Jason Zweig, and Warren E. Buffett

The Little Book of Common Sense Investing: The Only Way to Guarantee Your Fair Share of Stock Market Returns (Little Books. Big Profits) by John C. Bogle (Hardcover - Mar 5, 2007)

The Trouble with Mutual Funds by Richard Rutner, Financial Press, 2002.

Unconventional Success: A Fundamental Approach to Personal Investment, Free Press, 2005, by David Swensen

When I'm Sixty-Four: The Plot against Pensions and the Plan to Save Them by Teresa Ghilarducci (Hardcover - April 28, 2008)

Winning the Loser's Game, Fifth Edition: Timeless Strategies for Successful Investing by Charles Ellis (Hardcover - Oct 30, 2009)

OUTSTANDING ONLINE RESOURCES

401(k).org
   http://401k.org/
Investment Technologies
   http://www.investmenttechnologies.com/default.html

Center for Retirement Research at Boston College
    http://crr.bc.edu/
Vanguard retirement Portal
    https://retirementplans.vanguard.com/VGApp/pe/
    PubHome
Thrift Savings Plan
    http://www.tsp.gov/
The Pension Research Council
    http://www.pensionresearchcouncil.org/
Social Security Online
    www.socialsecurity.gov

ENDNOTES

1   Jones, Landon, *Great Expectations: America and the Baby Boom Generation*, New York: Coward, McCann and Geoghegan, 1980.

2   Ghilarducci, Teresa, *When I'm Sixty four: The Plot Against Pensions and the Plan to Save Them*, Princeton University Press, 2008, p. 8.

3   ibid, p. 11.

4   Babbel, David & Merrill, Craig, *Investing Your Lump Sum at Retirement*, Wharton Finanical Institution Policy Brief, August 14, 2007, p. 3.

5   *Annuity 2000 Mortality Table*, Society of Actuaries.

6   Babbel, David & Merill, Craig, op cit, p. 2.

7   Owram, Doug, *Born at the Right Time*, Toronto: Univ Of Toronto Press, 1997, p. x, and Jones, Landon, and *Great Expectations: America and the Baby Boom Generation*, New York: Coward, McCann and Geoghegan, 1980.

8   Mullins, Robert, *Baby Boomers Lag in Preparing Funerals, Estates*, The Business Journal of Milwaukee - December 18, 1998.

9   *Kicking and Screaming, Baby Boomers Begin to Talk About Aging*, The New York Times, March 30, 1998.

10 *Boomer Generation Is in a State of Denial*, Real Clear Politics, January 10, 2007.

11 *Employee Benefit Research Instituteís Retirement Confidence Survey*, 2006.

12 *Employee Benefit Research Instituteís Retirement Confidence Survey*, 2009.

13 The New York Post, Page 1, April 8, 2009.

14 *Spendthrift Boomers Face Perilous Retirement*, Dow Jones & Company, Inc. June 5, 2008.

15 *Talkiní íbout my generation: The economic impact of aging U.S. Baby Boomers*, Mckinsey Global Institute, Diana Farrell, Eric Beinhocker, Ezra Greenberg, Suruchi Shukla, Jonathan Ablett, and Geoffrey Greene, June, 2008.

16 *Many Baby Boomers Plan to Mix Work and Play*, About.com, Senior Living.

17 *Are Stocks Really Less Volatile in the Long Run?*, Lubos Pastor and Robert F. Stambaugh, National Bureau of Economic Research (NBER), May 22, 2009.

18 Shiller, Robert, *Irrational Exuberance, 2nd Ed., Random House*, 2005.

19 Wall Street Journal-Sponsored Investment Education Website

20 Edden, Roger, Evans, Richard, *Scale Effects in Mutual Fund Performance: The Role of Trading Costs*, March, 2007.

21 Transamerica Center for Retirement Studies, www.transamericacenter.org/resources.

22 Block, Sandra, *Traditional Company Pensions are Going Away Fast*, USA Today, May 22, 2009.

23 Ghilarducci, Teresa, *When Iím Sixty four, op cit*, 2008, P. 117-118.

24 *So Much for the 401(k). Now What?*, The New York Times, March 25, 2009.

25 *Employers Continue to Add Features to 401(k)s*, Money Management Executive, Editorial Staff, June 10, 2009.

26 Ghilarducci, Teresa, *When Iím Sixty four: op cit*, P. 117-131.

27 Nitolli Janice, *Now Is No Time to Skimp on Retirement Plans*, The Wall Street Journal, June, 2009.

28 *Staff Report Concerning Examinations of Select 401(k) Plan Consultants*, May 16, 2005.

29 Cunningham, Lawrence, and Buffett, Warren, *Essays of Warren Buffett*, 2002 ñ Import.

30 Bogle, John, *Common Sense on Mutual Funds: New Imperatives for the Intelligent Investor*, John Wiley & Sons, 2000.

31 Malkeil, Burton, *A Random Walk Down Wall Street: The Time-Tested Strategy for Successful Investing*, Revised and updated, W.W. Norton & Co, 2007.

32 Charles Ellis, *Winning The Loser's Game*, 5th ed., McGraw-Hill, 2002.

33 Benjamin Graham, *The Intelligent Investor*, Harper Collins, 1949, 2005.

34 Linnainmaa, Juhani *Understanding the Behavior of Uninformed Investors*, Capital Ideas, Chicago Booth, October, 2007.

35 Harry M. Markowitz, *Portfolio Selection*, New Haven, CT: Yale University Press, 1959.

36 White, Amanda, *Modern Portfolio Theory still holds up, Harry Markowitz Says So*, Top 1000 Funds, Summer, 2009.

37 Swensen, David, *Unconventional Success: A Fundamental Approach to Personal Investment*, Free Press, 2005.

I invite you to visit my web site:

WWW.NEWRETIREMENTREALITIES.COM

CPSIA information can be obtained at www.ICGtesting.com
Printed in the USA
LVOW08s1500010813

345833LV00001B/42/P